SPEEDWALKING

The
Exercise
Alternative

SPEEDWALKING

Lilian Rowen
and
D. S. Laiken

G. P. PUTNAM'S SONS   NEW YORK

Copyright © 1980 by Lilian Rowen and D. S. Laiken

All rights reserved. This book, or parts thereof, may not be reproduced in any form without permission. Published simultaneously in Canada by Academic Press Canada Limited, Toronto.

Illustrations by Mady Kraus

Designed by Mary Jane Dimassi

Library of Congress Cataloging in Publication Data

Rowen, Lilian.
  Speedwalking.

  1. Walking (Sports)   I. Laiken, Deidre S., joint
author. II. Title.
GV1071.R68   1980   613.7′1   80-13355
ISBN 0-399-12526-4

Printed in the United States of America

ACKNOWLEDGMENTS:

I am especially grateful to the following people:

Dr. Hans Kraus, who encouraged me and believed in the idea of speedwalking.

Dr. David T. Mininberg, who patiently helped me with the development of my flexibility exercises.

The California Walkers, who generously shared their time and thoughts.

Drs. Nesrin Bingol and Paul Salkin, who so generously lent me their spacious house and grounds to prepare this book.

Deidre Laiken, my coauthor, whose patience and understanding made this project a pleasure and a success.

And last, but never least, my husband Mel, whose constant support keeps me going.

LILIAN ROWEN
New York City
February 1980

To all my students whose support and affection throughout the years made this book possible. And to my agent, Wendy Lipkind, who helped me bring it all together.

LILIAN ROWEN

CONTENTS

SPEEDWALKING

1.
SPEEDWALKING

WHAT IS IT?

It's not walking. It's not running. It's something everyone can do—and doing it will tone your muscles, slim your waist, flatten your stomach, increase the aerobic capacity of your heart and lungs, *and* make you feel terrific. It's called "Speed-walking." It will succeed where other exercises have failed. That's because speedwalking is life-preserving and life-enhancing. It doesn't take hours of grueling discipline, nor is there an agonizing "wall of pain" to confront.

Speedwalking gets you moving and keeps you moving. Whether you're a running dropout, a perpetual dieter, an exercise-hater, or an "armchair athlete," you'll find that speedwalking is a sport that fits into your life. It's the exercise alternative everyone's been waiting for.

WHY SPEEDWALK?

Speedwalking is different from all the other exercises you've tried or have refused to try. I've created it especially to meet your needs: the need to feel fit, look trim, and stay in shape without worrying about accidents or injuries. I know about these needs because I share them. After injuring my knee while jogging, I began to look for an outdoor exercise to replace my daily runs in the park. It wasn't easy. Ordinary walking was too slow. It failed to give me the physical or psychological boost that running did. As a director of an exercise studio with twenty-five years of experience, I knew that walking just couldn't provide the all-over body benefits of a well-balanced calisthenics program.

I was looking for an outdoor activity that was relatively injury-free, one that was exhilarating, and one that also promoted flexibility and stamina. In short, I was looking for the complete exercise. My clients, men and women who lead busy, demanding lives, were looking for it too.

My search led me to Europe where I participated in the Olympic sport of race walking, which impressed me as a terrific way to tone up arms, legs, hips, and stomach. Race walking needed no expensive equipment and could be done almost anywhere. It was just too demanding and strenuous for the average person, however. That's when I came up with the perfect solution—and the perfect exercise.

I decided to adapt and modify the old sport of race walking in order to create a new exercise—one that would tone, shape, and slim without causing damage to bones or aggravating stiffness in the joints. Most important, I wanted this to be an exercise that everyone could do because it was fun and easy to fit into a hectic schedule. And that's how the sport of speed-walking was born.

Speedwalking is an updated version of race walking. It's less strenuous and less exaggerated than race walking, and can be practiced by a greater variety of people. And the good news is that speedwalking eliminates thunderous jolts to the spine and dangerous pounding of legs, feet, and ankles that have caused so many jogging injuries (and dropouts). When you speedwalk, both feet are never in the air simultaneously. That's because, like all walking, speedwalking consists of a progression of steps that maintain unbroken contact with the ground at all times. Unlike ordinary walking, however, speedwalking involves total body motion. This means that every time you speedwalk, you'll be getting a *total body exercise* because you'll be working every major muscle group. The result—a coordinated series of movements that won't overuse particular sets of muscles while underusing others.

Speedwalking is an extraordinary exercise. In one easy-to-learn combination of foot, leg, hip, and arm movements, it gives you the benefits of at least a half dozen different exercises. This makes your fitness program a lot easier, faster, and more effective. Each time you speedwalk, you can be sure you're getting a complete, well-balanced, and *safe* workout.

HOW DOES A SPEEDWALKING PROGRAM WORK?

As an exercise instructor, I know that no matter how much you want to begin an activity program, it's not always easy. Sometimes the reason is psychological—past failure, embarrassment, or just the notion that certain exercises are beyond your ability. Other times, the reason is clearly physical. If you've been sedentary for several months or years, have been a "weekend athlete" or an exercise-hater, you'll need to stretch and stimulate "sleeping" muscles before you undertake a new activity. This is why I've devised a special speedwalking program. I want you to begin speedwalking with the confidence that you'll continue for the rest of your life. And that's not an unrealistic commitment, because you can speedwalk to work, before work, on your lunch break, or with family and friends on the weekends. Wherever and whenever you used to walk, you can now SPEEDWALK!

The speedwalking program begins with a special get-ready week, seven days of confidence building, muscle strengthening, and flexibility enhancement. In this first week, you'll pinpoint your individual weak spots and learn how to strengthen them *before* you begin regular speedwalking. These seven days will give you time to get your mind *and* your body ready for a completely new experience. They'll help you ease yourself into a routine of exercise that's practical *and* effective.

Once you're ready to go out and speedwalk, you'll need to learn the proper warm-ups and cool-downs to keep you flexible and relaxed. Chapters 4 and 5 provide a program of exercises that only take a few minutes and are tailored specifically to your speedwalking routine.

When you're warmed-up *and* psyched-up, you're ready for Chapter 3, which explains and illustrates the complete technique of speedwalking, including do's and don'ts to stop bad habits before they begin.

What about diet, equipment, and your individual problems? It's all here—all part of a special program designed for real people—people who want to stay fit, slim, and healthy without having to devote all their time and energy to difficult and/or demanding exercises. My coauthor, a sports and fitness writer, and I have thought of all your needs. Even the need for encouragement. In Chapter 6, you'll find special tips to get you going and keep you going (yes, everyone feels like dropping out once in a while). Whether your goal is weight loss, improved muscle tone, increased aerobic efficiency, or just the need to lead a more active life, these goals are all just a few speedwalking steps away.

2.
YOUR GET-READY WEEK

You've probably heard the expression; "Don't play a sport to get in shape. Get in shape to play a sport." For strenuous and demanding activities this is imperative—and for speedwalking, it's good advice. Although most anyone can begin speedwalking once they've mastered the basic technique, it's a good idea to take a week to get ready. This time is used to locate your weak spots and to begin stretching and strengthening all your muscles before beginning an intensive speedwalking program. This get-ready week is designed to give you an important physical *and* psychological edge. Sore muscles and deflated egos are often the result of plunging weak and unconditioned muscles into a sudden and dramatic fitness program. For most of us, taking things slowly and carefully reduces discouragement, minimizes charley horse, and improves performance— vital keys to continued motivation and enthusiastic participation.

If you're one of the lucky few who have managed to remain flexible and active over the years, you won't experience much soreness with these get-ready exercises. If you've been inactive for some time, however, you're bound to feel some mild muscle aches and soreness once you begin exercising. Those aches and pains are only temporary and are a natural result of using old muscles in new ways. By spending a week (or more) preparing yourself, you'll actually reduce or eliminate a severe charley horse later on. My prescription for any annoying soreness? A few hot baths, a friendly massage, and the determination to stick with it. The soreness will disappear in a day or two.

The get-ready week begins with a simple strength and flexibility test to help you locate weak areas—areas that you'll want especially to prepare for speedwalking. Chances are, you already know if you have weak stomach muscles, but you're probably unaware of your shoulder and hip joint flexibility. These areas are important for speedwalking, since they increase your stride *and* your speed. Hamstring and leg muscle flexibility is essential too. The muscles in the back of your legs rarely get the stretch they need in everyday activities such as walking, or even in jogging. No matter what your age or physical condition, it's important that you get a regular physical examination and that you check with your doctor about the advisability of any new activity.

MAKING THIS WEEK WORK FOR YOU!

After you've completed the simple strength and flexibility test, you should have a fairly good idea what areas of your body will need special attention. You can then choose the exercises in the get-ready program that will stretch and strengthen those areas. If you've been sedentary for a year or more, stick with the single-starred exercises. Double-starred exercises are a bit more advanced. The whole program takes between twenty and thirty minutes and should be done at least five times a week.

Most people prefer to set aside a full week for this get-ready program, but you should work at your own speed. If you feel you'd like more conditioning time, you can take longer and stay with this program a few more days. It's also a good idea to take brisk daily walks to build stamina during this week.

Preparing yourself for a new physical activity should also involve some mental exercise. You might want to take time during this week to set realistic goals for yourself—such as weight loss or better muscle tone or increased flexibility. You'll also want to plan when, and how, you'll fit a regular program of speedwalking into your own schedule. A haphazard activity program will not give you the results and the feeling of well-being that a well-planned, realistically scheduled one will. When you do set up a schedule, be sure to set aside "make-up time" in case you should happen to miss a workout due to unexpected events, bad weather, or illness. (See Chapter 6 for tips on setting goals and making schedules.)

It's also possible that after only one week of regular exercise you'll discover that certain areas, such as stomach and leg muscles, need a bit more conditioning time. If this is the case, you can choose a few exercises and do them as supplements to your regular speedwalking. During bad weather, or at times when you can't get out to speedwalk, why not stay inside and do a full twenty- or thirty-minute exercise routine? The idea is to tailor this program to *your* needs. Finding your weak spots is the first step. Strengthening and conditioning them will take time, but you'll be surprised at how quickly your body responds. Keeping up with this program on your "off days" is not only a great way to stay in terrific speedwalking shape—it will also help you maintain the progress you've achieved.

THE SPEEDWALKER'S
STRENGTH AND FLEXIBILITY TEST

This test is quick and easy, but it will give you a good indication which areas need special attention.

You can then concentrate on exercises that condition these specific areas. The first two exercises were taken from the Kraus-Weber test, a test designed by Doctors Hans Kraus and Sonia Weber that measures strength and flexibility of the large posture muscles. The other two exercises have been used sucessfully in my clinics and classes. Don't be upset or surprised if you can't complete a position—most people have

Speedwalkers being tested for hip and waist flexibility.
Photo by Truman Moore

difficulty with at least one, and some with all four. The reason for this is that in our daily lives we rarely get a chance to stretch and strengthen all the basic muscle groups. Even if you can't complete all these exercises don't be discouraged; you'll just need to give problem areas more concentrated attention. The exercises in the get-ready program are designed to deal with common weak spots. Doing them every week will result in a marked improvement in a very short time. Remember, just because you haven't used these muscles, don't think that they have disappeared. They're just waiting for you to put them back to work again!

1. Bent-Knee Sit-Up

This is a good test for abdominal strength. Remember that strong abdominal muscles help support your back and lessen backaches.

Begin by lying on your back with bent knees; your feet should be anchored beneath a desk or chair. Your hands should be behind your head. Slowly curl up to a sitting position—chin to chest. You can bring your elbows forward to help yourself sit up. Do this once. YOUR EVENTUAL GOAL IS TO SIT UP.

2.Floor Touch

This is one way to measure the flexibility of your spine and the muscles in back of your thighs (hamstring muscles).

From a standing position, slowly reach down as far as you can and try to touch the floor. Don't jerk. Move slowly. If you can't get all the way down, go just as far as you can. Do this once. YOUR EVENTUAL GOAL IS TO TOUCH THE FLOOR WITH YOUR FINGERTIPS.

3.Shoulder Flex

This will tell you just how flexible your shoulder girdle is. Strong upper arms and shoulders are important in speedwalking, since they will increase your momentum. These muscles also have an effect on your everyday posture.

Bend both arms at the elbows. Reach your left arm over your left shoulder and bring your right arm around your back and stretch it upward. If you are really flexible you will be able to grasp the fingers (or even the wrists) of the opposite hands. Repeat this exercise by switching arm positions. Don't be surprised if you can do the complete posture on one side, but not on the other. It's normal to be more flexible and/or stronger on one side. Do this once on each side. YOUR EVENTUAL GOAL IS TO TOUCH THE FINGERTIPS OF THE OPPOSITE HANDS.

4.Hip Girdle Flex

Since men usually have less flexibility in this area, they will have more difficulty with this exercise. The hip joint area also becomes less flexible with age, but this can be remedied with continued exercise. Long strides are important in speedwalking. Building flexibility in this area will help you move more gracefully and more swiftly.

Sit on the floor. Straighten the left leg out and keep the right leg as perpendicular to it as possible without straining. At first you might only get your leg in the position marked by dotted lines on the figure. Sit up straight and keep your arms directly out in front of you. Hold for a count of five. Repeat on the

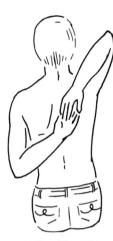

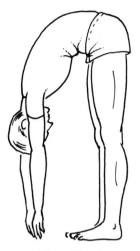

Floor Touch

Shoulder Flex

Hip Girdle Flex

opposite side. Do this once. YOUR EVENTUAL GOAL IS TO SIT UP STRAIGHT WITH YOUR ARMS OUT IN FRONT OF YOU.

LOOKING AT YOUR TEST RESULTS

The results of this test probably surprised you. Even if you have been fairly active, chances are you lack flexibility in at least one of these areas. Before you proceed with the get-ready exercises, make a note of those areas that will need special attention. Every exercise in the program is geared to one or more of these areas, so you can concentrate on your *individual weak spots*.

If the test showed that you need to work on all four areas, this doesn't mean that you have "failed" anything. It just indicates that the exercises you have been doing have not been balanced, or that you have not been active enough. To get in shape, just proceed with the get-ready program by doing every single-starred exercise at least three to five times (unless otherwise indicated). Remember that this test was only meant to point up weak areas. It does not mean that you can't speed-walk. Many of these weak areas will become stronger and more flexible during your daily speedwalking workouts or as you practice your warm-ups and cool-downs. As a matter of fact, try retaking this test after three months of daily speedwalking. This time you'll be a lot more pleased with the results!

THE GET-READY EXERCISES

*A single asterisk indicates that an exercise is for beginners and should be done three to five times, unless otherwise indicated.

**A double asterisk indicates that an exercise involves a greater degree of difficulty and should only be tried after you have mastered the single-starred exercises.

1. The Total Relaxers*

These simple exercises are a must for everyone. They only take a minute or two but they help you relax those tense muscles. This makes stretching easier and exercising more enjoyable.

Assume the basic position—lie on your back, knees bent, feet on the floor, legs comfortably apart.

(a) Take three deep breaths. Place your hand on your lower abdomen as you inhale slowly. Notice that your abdomen will expand slightly—like a balloon. Exhale through your mouth. (b) Now, slowly pull your shoulders up toward your ears—make sure you keep them on the floor, simply drag them upward. As you exhale, push your shoulders downward. Do this three times. (c) Gently roll your head from side to side. Do this three times to each side. (d) Finally, bring both knees slowly up to your chest and hold them there for thirty seconds. RELAX.

These tension relievers work best in a quiet atmosphere when your eyes are closed and you're able to escape the pressures of the day.

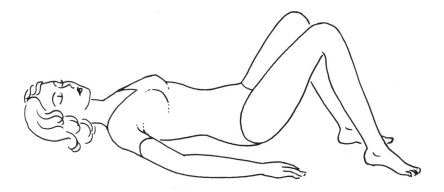

2. The High Roller*

This simple exercise tones the abdominal muscles while it stretches the spine.

Assume the basic position. Slowly bring your knees up to your chest. Return to the starting position. Roll your knees up again, only this time lift your hips off the floor. Return to the basic position. Try this two more times, rolling backward as much as you can (note dotted lines on figure, left).

3. Semi-Sit-Up*

This is an effective way to strengthen and tone your abdominal muscles.

Assume the basic position. Tuck chin to chest, round your back, and lift your shoulder blades slowly off the floor. Your arms and hands should be extended directly over your knees. Do this three to five times.

4. Waist Twister*

Here's an easy way to tone your hips and limber up your waist.

Lie on your back, with knees to chest. Place your arms out at shoulder level. Let both knees drop gently to your right side. Using your stomach muscles, pull your knees up to your chest

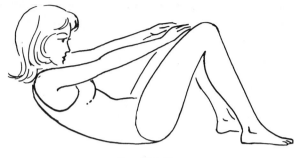

Semi-Sit-Up

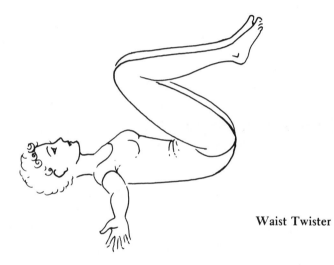

Waist Twister

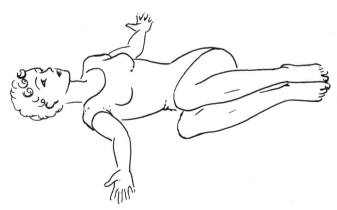

and drop them gently to your left side. Make sure both shoulders always remain on the floor. Begin by doing this exercise six times to each side, alternating sides; then progress to twelve times.

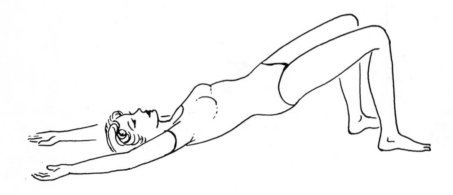

5. The Bridge*

This is a terrific way to increase flexibility in the hips and shoulders.

Assume the basic position. Lift your hips off the floor as high as you can, while you stretch your arms overhead. Hold this position for a slow count of five. Now slowly roll your spine back to the starting position. You should roll back, vertebra by vertebra, from the top of your spine. Your arms will return to the original position as you roll back. Do this three times.

6. The Bridge Split**

Here is a more advanced exercise for hip and inner thigh flexibility.

Lie on your back. With the soles of your feet together, and your thighs wide apart, slowly lift your hips as high as possible off the floor. Hold for a slow count of five. Return to the original position. Do this three times.

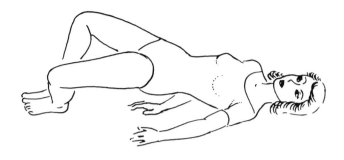

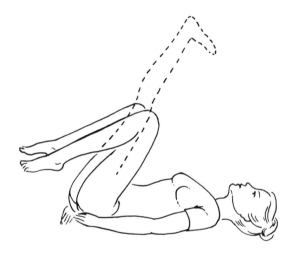

7.Single Heel Stretch*

This is an important exercise because it stretches those muscles in the back of your legs.

Lie on your back, knees to chest, your hands placed under your buttocks, palms down. Slowly stretch your right leg toward the ceiling with your heel pushing upward. Hold to a count of three. Bend your knee, and repeat with your left leg. It's important to keep both knees pressed together during this stretch, even if at first you're unable to straighten either leg. Do this three times with each leg, alternating legs.

The Praying Mantis

8. The Praying Mantis**

Here's an all-over leg exercise; it strengthens ankles and stretches shins and thighs.

Flex your knees and bring them toward your chest. Put the soles of your feet together and keep your knees wide apart. Slowly straighten your legs out, while the soles of your feet remain together. Only straighten your knees as far as you can without separating your feet. Do this three to five times.

9. Quad Stretcher**

The quadriceps are those muscles in the front of your thighs. This is a good way to stretch them and prepare yourself for speedwalking.

Assume the basic position. Grasp both ankles. Slowly ease your right knee toward the floor. Return to the starting position. Repeat with your left knee. You may not be able to touch the floor at first, but you should feel that stretch in your quadriceps. Alternating, do this six times to each side.

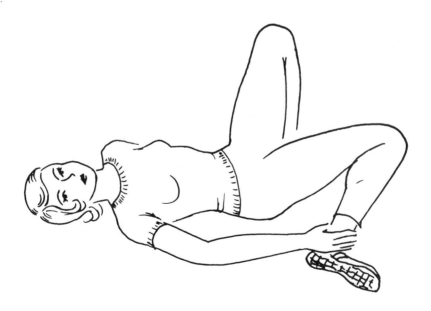

10.Spread Eagle*

You'll find that this exercise really tightens and tones those abdominal muscles.

Lie on your back, legs apart, arms overhead, comfortably apart. Now bring your right arm and left leg together so they touch. Return to starting position. Repeat with the left arm and right leg. This exercise should always be done slowly and smoothly. Alternating, repeat four to six times on each side.

11. The Swinger**

This is an effective way to increase flexibility in the shoulders and hips—flexibility you'll need every time you speedwalk!

Lie on your right side. Swing your left leg forward while your left arm swings backward. Then swing the leg backward, while the arm swings forward. Swing back and forth six to ten times. Then turn onto your left side and repeat with your right arm and leg.

12. The Total Sit-Up**

The sit-up is a classic exercise for abdominal strength—that's because it works! Always keep your knees bent to avoid back problems. Keep your hands by your sides, and hook your ankles under a heavy object. Slowly curl up until your chin touches your knees. Return slowly to starting position. It's important that you keep your heels close to your buttocks. If you have trouble with the sit-up, stay with the "Semi-Sit-Up" for a while. Start by doing this three times and work up to ten times.

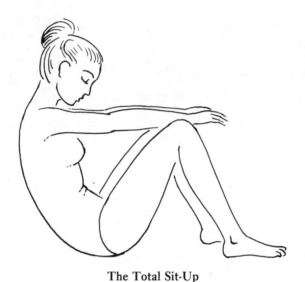

The Total Sit-Up

13. The Swivel*

Most of us could use some additional flexibility in the hip girdle area—here's a great way to get it.

Get in a sitting position. Lean back on your hands and bend your arms at the elbows. Your left leg should be straight out in front of you. Bend your right knee so that your right foot is next to your left thigh. Then lift your right leg and turn it in, so that the right knee touches the floor close to your left thigh. Keeping the right leg bent, repeat the movement three to five times. Then straighten the right leg and swivel with the left leg.

The Swivel

14. The Airplane*

This simple movement will keep your waist strong, slim, and flexible.

Stand with your legs comfortably apart. Keep your arms out at shoulder level. Bend forward and point your right arm toward the ceiling. Your left arm will point downward. Reverse the position, twisting from side to side. Keep your eyes upward, toward the ceiling. Repeat six times each side.

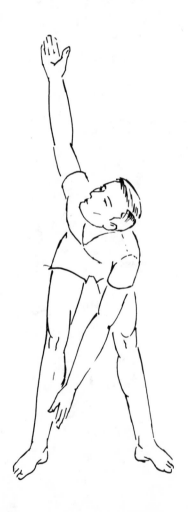

15. The Arm Crisscross*

More shoulder flexibility will give you more momentum when you speedwalk. Here's one more way to increase yours.

Stand with your legs comfortably apart. Bend forward. Cross your arms. Keeping the same position, swing your arms upward and try crossing them behind your back. Repeat five to ten times.

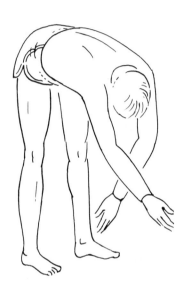

3.
OUT AND WALKING

My interest in speedwalking has taken me to Europe and across the United States. People everywhere are looking for an exercise alternative and I was looking for the people who believed they had found it. My interest in these people was sparked by Dr. George Sheehan, a cardiologist and marathon runner. In his well-known book, *Dr. Sheehan on Running*, he describes race walkers as "part of a ground-swell that may become the wave of the future." He goes on to explain the reasons:

"The race walker, for one thing, can make do with ordinary feet. He can put miles and miles on feet that would break down in any other sport. And he isn't likely to get injuries further up in the kinetic chain that goes from foot to leg to knee to thigh to low back. Race walking is virtually injury free . . .

"The main source of this protection is the walker's swivel-hipped form. This prevents bounce and largely cancels out any shock on impact. His foot plant—starting with the heel, riding along the outside of the foot and delivering straight ahead, is just what the Creator planned. And the locked knee, a race walking requirement, keeps the kneecap in its appropriate place, the patellar groove, thus preventing the too-frequent knee problems seen in runners, tennis players and other athletes."*

Just to see if Dr. Sheehan's findings were accurate, I went to UCLA and spent a few sunny summer weeks walking, talking, and sharing information with some of the country's most experienced and enthusiastic race walkers. In only a few days, I

Lilian Rowen speedwalking on U.C.L.A. campus with the California Walkers. From left to right: John Kelly, Paula Kash, Roger Brandwein, Lilian Rowen, and Malory Geller. *Photo By Kurt Meissner*

* George A. Sheehan, M.D., *Dr. Sheehan on Running*, (Mt. View, CA.: World Publications, 1975), p. 42.

found that many of these dedicated race walkers had once been dedicated runners. Injuries and boredom had turned them away from daily runs and persuaded them to try daily walks instead.

John Kelly, AAU Race Walk Chairman and the coach of the California Walkers, a group dedicated to this sport, and one whose membership is growing daily, began walking in 1965 after he suffered a bad Achilles tendon pull while running. A robust fifty-year-old, Kelly won the Santa Monica thirteen-mile half-marathon with an impressive finishing time of one hour, fifty-three minutes and thirty-seven seconds. John really enjoys race walking and judging from the terrific shape he's in, it's a sport he'll be participating in for a long time!

Roger Brandwein, an Olympic race walking hopeful, switched from running because he was looking for a sport with more body motion, concentration, and challenge. Paula Kash, another top California race walker, feels that this sport combines dance, gymnastics, and running. After watching Paula walk, I felt as though I had just witnessed the graceful, fluid performance of a ballerina.

Don't get the idea that all race walkers (and speedwalkers) are running dropouts. Forty-year-old Jan Geller took up the sport to improve her physical condition and to keep up with her thirty-two-year-old runner husband. The result—she looks and feels terrific, and she has even converted her husband to walking (he recently walked a twenty-six-mile Santa Monica marathon)!

Many people take up a sport to lose weight. If weight loss is your goal (along with fitness, I hope!), here's some good news from race walker Terry Mathews: He's found that after race walking ten miles he loses more weight than when he runs the same distance!

Spending time with these determined walkers convinced me that race walking was more than a substitute for running—it was a superior sport. I also knew that it demanded a great deal of upper body strength and lower back flexibility. That's why I made some adaptations and created speedwalking. You see, not all of my students are running dropouts. Many are simply exercise-haters. They feel they are too old, too out of shape, or just too weak to try anything more demanding than sitting down and getting up again. But believe me, speedwalking has converted even the most dedicated exercise-hater.

One particular young man, Bill Hersh, a thirty-six-year-old accountant, had hardly exercised at all in five years. He explained his attitude this way: "It seems like everyone is in constant 'pain,' trying to break running records and enter twenty-six-mile marathons. I need a sport that can make me feel like a superstar even if I don't run a four (or even eight) minute mile."

After only three weeks of regular speedwalking, Bill began to see and feel the results. He lost five pounds and had more energy and enthusiasm for everything he did. To Bill's surprise, he did become a "speedwalking superstar" after all. Today he is learning how to race walk and intends to enter an upcoming marathon.

Making the transition from speedwalking to race walking isn't mandatory, but if you too should become a "superstar," there's no reason why you can't try this more demanding sport. The Appendix will give you the information you'll need to make the transition.

BEFORE YOU TAKE THAT FIRST STEP

Now that you're flexible and motivated, it's time to learn the complete speedwalking technique. Here are just a few helpful guidelines to remember each time you practice:

1. Always warm up and cool down before and after each workout. This prevents injury.

2. Speedwalking styles look different because everyone's body is different. If you have long legs, your stride will be longer. More flexibility in the hips will give you an even longer stride. Arm movements vary and it's always best to find what's most comfortable for you. Every speedwalker develops his or her own style. Keep this in mind when you walk. Even though

Everyone here is speedwalking with a slightly different style.
Photo by Truman Moore

someone else may look different than you, it doesn't necessarily mean that you're doing anything wrong.

3. Always wear soft, low-heeled, flexible shoes or, preferably, running shoes (for more on how to select footwear, see pp. 103–106.

4. If you're over forty, have any particular physical problems, or have been inactive for an extended period of time, please check with your doctor before you begin this program— and then take it slow and easy.

5. *Remember, speedwalking is fun! Enjoy it!*

TECHNIQUE

Feet First

The heel-toe movement is a vital part of speedwalking. It's important to master this first and to practice it whenever

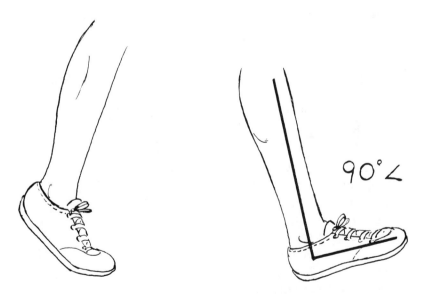

Heel planted on the ground with foot at 90° angle to shin.

you're wearing low-heeled shoes. Practice this simple movement when you're walking to work or just taking a stroll (one
woman uses it when she's rushing to catch a bus!). Once
mastered, it will feel quite natural and you won't even have to
think about it as you speedwalk.

To begin, plant your heel firmly on the ground. Place it so
that your foot is at a 90 degree angle to your shin. Roll your
foot forward, keeping your weight on the outside of the foot

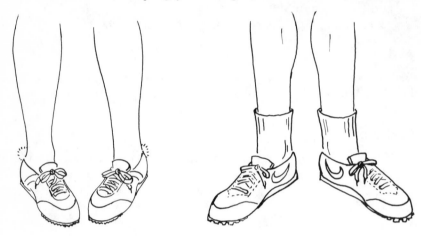

"Toeing In" and "Toeing Out"

until you feel a slight pressure on your toes. Also check to
make sure that you're not bouncing up and down on your feet
as you heel-toe. Be careful to point your foot forward and place
it in a straight position rather than "toeing in" or out (see
illustration above. If you naturally toe in or out, it's important to adjust your foot placement as you walk. At first this
heel-toe technique may cause a charley horse in the shin
and/or calf muscles. Here's a terrific way to get some relief if
you start to ache! Sit back on your heels for one minute. This
will stretch the muscles that have been contracted during the
heel-toe movement. Don't bounce! Just sit still and feel that
s-t-r-e-t-c-h. (This is the "Shin Stretcher," one of the cool-
down techniques; see p. 79.)

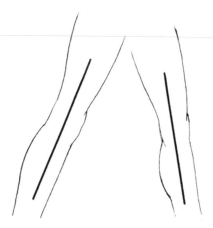

Straightening forward (left) knee, keeping back leg (right knee) straight as long as possible.

Thigh Technique

For many people, the thigh technique is the most difficult movement to master. That's because it often means "unlearning" something we all do when we walk—bend both knees at the same time. In order to get the desired speed, however, it's important that you keep your back leg straight.

Using the heel-toe movement, put your left leg forward. Just before the heel makes contact with the ground, straighten your left knee. Pull backward vigorously with your front thigh (you'll feel this pulling in your quadriceps, or thigh muscle). While this is happening, your back leg will be swinging through to take the next step. Keep the back leg straight as long as possible. It should feel as if the strong push-pull of your forward leg is pulling your rear leg off the ground. One way to get this feeling is to speedwalk up a slight incline. You'll be able to feel that front leg pulling you up the hill. Walking downhill at this time will be difficult, so use the incline as a way to practice your technique.

Start your stride by planting your left heel firmly on the gound, your foot at a 90 degree angle with shin, and back leg straight. *Photo by Truman Moore*

Left thigh pulling, right knee driving through. *Photo by Truman Moore*

Full stride extension. Forward leg pulling rear leg off the ground. *Photo by Truman Moore*

Muscle Awareness

Many of my students and friends have questions about the "locked knee" aspect of speedwalking. They aren't sure if, or when, they're using their quadriceps properly. Since most people don't even know where these muscles are, here's an exercise designed to help you locate your quadriceps, to experience the "locked knee," and to experience the feeling of your quads contracting correctly. By the way, the quadriceps are those muscles that give your thighs shape. As you master this technique and continue to practice it, you will notice a marked improvement in the shape of your thighs.

Lie on your back on the floor. Put your hand on your left thigh. Now, straighten your left knee completely. Your hand will feel a slight hardening of the thigh as the muscle contracts. Those muscles are your quadriceps and that's exactly how they should work when you practice the locked knee technique. If you have any trouble with this technique when you're out speedwalking, visualize yourself doing this simple exercise. Isolate your quadriceps in your mind's eye and it will all come back to you!

Combining Foot and Thigh Movements

Once you've mastered the heel-toe movement and the thigh technique, spend a week or so combining both these movements until you have a slow and fluid walk. DON'T WORK FOR SPEED AT THIS TIME. Concentrate on proper technique. This is the time to build good habits and to check your foot alignment as you walk slowly. Once you feel that your leading leg is straight and pulling you forward, the walk will accelerate by itself. You will automatically feel yourself picking up speed and a certain rhythm. When this begins to happen, you're ready for the next three components of speedwalking.

Hip Swivel

The hip swivel should not be a highly exaggerated movement. It should not be a "wiggle" or a "shake." But since everyone

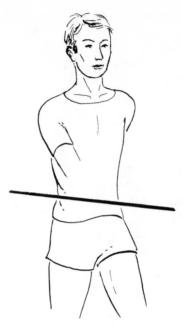

Walking from the hip.

has a different degree of flexibility in this area, some people will appear to have a more distinct swivel than others. Just imagine yourself "walking from the hip." Turn your hip in slightly as you swing your leg forward.

As you walk more and more and continue to practice the hip girdle flexibility exercises (see "Bumps and Grinds" on p. 62), you'll find that your leg is swinging out further and your stride is longer. But don't push it. Try for a natural swivel and avoid any bouncing and wiggling.

If you should get a stitch in your side while practicing, take a few deep breaths and slow down. If the stitch becomes more severe, turn to pp. 53–54 for advice and exercises that can help to prevent this condition. Because of the swivel movement, it's important to avoid tight waistbands and to reduce intake of foods and liquids just prior to speedwalking. (For more about what to eat and what to wear, see Chapter 7, "Special Needs.")

Head, Neck, and Torso Position

Your torso and head should be held in a nearly upright position. Never lean backward. Try to relax your upper body and shoulders. The correct position should feel as if your torso were "sitting on your pelvis." Because you're outdoors and moving, you'll probably be tempted to turn your head to take in the scenery. Try to keep head movement to a minimum, however. Your head and neck should be kept straight, but not rigid. Relax this area and minimize sideways movement.

Of course, if you're walking where there's traffic, or other distractions, you will have to remain aware of what's going on around you. For this reason, it might be a good idea to pick a familiar route when you're first learning to speedwalk. With few distractions, you'll be able to keep your head and neck aligned and your spine straight. These habits will help you to build speed and fluidity later on.

Arm Movement

Like the hip swivel, arm motion will vary from individual to individual. There are a few basic rules, however.

As in regular walking, your arms should swing in the direction opposite to your legs. In other words, when your right leg steps forward, your left arm should swing in the same direction, and vice versa. Bend your arms slightly at the elbow and keep them fairly close to your body.

Flailing your arms can slow you down, and it can be a hazard to other people as well. Don't lift your shoulders or swing them from side to side. Exaggerated arm movements are more characteristic of race walking. When done in speedwalking, these movements can lead to uncomfortable tension and pain around the shoulder girdle. Relax your arms and let them swing comfortably. You'll move along at a nice steady pace and you won't pay the price with aches and pains later on!

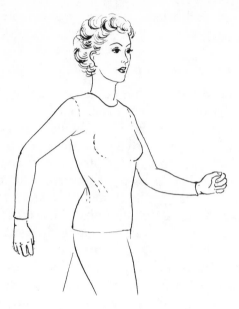

Arms slightly bent, held fairly close to the body.

PUTTING IT ALL TOGETHER

Now that you know all the separate components of speedwalking, it's time to put them together and get out there and walk! It's not really an effort to combine separate movements, however, since they all work together and it only takes a few trial walks to get your body moving with fluidity, grace, and ease.

As you walk, think about the correct technique. DON'T BE CONCERNED ABOUT SPEED. Go slowly and easily. Check your foot alignment from time to time and make sure your arms are close to your body and your shoulders aren't lifting or shaking. Your body should be fairly straight, with the hips swiveling slightly. You might feel some discomfort in your shins or ankles as you heel-toe along. If the discomfort begins to build, slow down and walk regularly for a few steps (see "Variety Walking," pp. 57–58).

You might get a stitch in your side. This really is harmless and is caused by a spasm in the diaphragm. A slight stitch can

This how you should look when you put hip, arm and thigh movement together correctly. *Photo by Truman Moore*

be relieved by slowing down and breathing deeply. More severe pain is usually a result of improper breathing habits. Here's a good way to practice proper breathing habits and to prevent an annoying stitch.

HOW TO IMPROVE YOUR BREATH CONTROL

When people first start a new physical activity they tend to tense up and take short and fast breaths instead of breathing deeply and slowly. This leads to quick exhaustion and sometimes to a "stitch." Take some time to practice the "Deep Breath" and you will automatically take deeper and slower breaths when you exert yourself physically.

I suggest practicing before you go to sleep because deep breathing acts as a sedative and helps you fall asleep.

Here's how: Lie flat on your back. Place one hand on your rib cage and the other on your belly. Breathe in very gradually through your nose. (If you take in too much air too quickly, it cuts your breath short.) Very slow inhalation will enable you to take in the large amount of oxygen needed for physical exertion. Start with a timespan of five seconds of inhalation and work your way up to ten seconds. (A second is usually accepted as being the time it takes to say one thousand and one, one thousand and two, etc.) As you inhale slowly you should feel your rib cage expand and your belly push *outward*. Hold your breath for a moment, then start exhaling just as gradually through the mouth, eventually aiming for a timespan of twelve seconds. Exhalation should always take longer than inhalation. Repeat a few times until you feel a "Yen to Yawn." This is very relaxing and a good way to fall asleep.

WHAT AM I DOING WRONG?

At first you may not be sure if you've "got it." Speedwalking is rhythmic and natural—it's actually the basic walking motion refined and perfected. Any distorted, exaggerated movement is one indication that you're doing something wrong, or that you're overdoing a specific technique. But it does take time. It helps if you can have someone else observe you and check the instructions on the previous pages as you walk.

In addition, study the photographs of speedwalkers on pp. 41, 44, 53, and 70–71. Although individual styles vary, all these people are using proper arm, torso, hip, leg, and foot techniques. Although you may not have taken up speedwalking to win awards for form, correct technique *is* important. It will give you the best results, will keep you moving at a rapid, rhythmic pace, and will help to prevent injury. Incorrect technique adds stress to speedwalking, multiplies aches and pains, and can actually contribute to disappointing results.

Here is a convenient checklist of common problems *and* effective solutions. Again, if you can, enlist someone to observe you while you walk. If for some reason this isn't possible, be aware of each of these mistakes and observe yourself. Check your form as you're walking and continue to spot-check yourself as you progress. It's much easier to correct problems when you first begin to speedwalk than it is later on, after they have become ingrained habits.

1.Arms Too High

Holding your arms up too high hurts! It leads to a tense upper body and quick fatigue of arms and torso. Here are some indications you are not keeping your arms at the correct height:
- Your arms are extremely tense and are pumping vigorously.
- Your elbows are bent at greater than a 90 degree angle. To correct this problem:
- Walk with your arms folded on your chest or with your hands grasped at the small of your back.
- Practice relaxing your shoulders, even when you are moving rapidly.
- Concentrate on developing the proper arm swing, by isolating this movement and practicing it by itself.

2.Improper Head Position

Tilting your head too far forward or back is a common speedwalking error. Here's how to detect this flaw in your technique:
- You feel tension and fatigue in your upper back and chest.
- If you're leaning forward too much, you'll be pulling the trailing foot away too soon.
- You feel persistent neck aches after each workout. To prevent this problem from becoming an ingrained habit:
- Keep your eyes fixed on a point on the ground, about ten feet directly in front of you.
- Work on relaxing your neck and upper body.
- Visualize the proper head position before you begin speedwalking.

3. Improper Foot Alignment

"Toeing in," "toeing out," or even crossing one foot over the other are bothersome habits. Here are some ways to check yourself for these mistakes:

- Your body "lifts" or bounces as you walk. Sometimes both feet almost lift off the ground.
- You don't achieve the full hip movement.
- You're not achieving a full stride.

Although you may not be able to overcome this problem completely, you can decrease it by watching yourself carefully. Here are some ways to help yourself:

- Walk on sand or a soft surface and examine your footprints; you'll then become more aware of your foot position.
- Walk on a lane marker or some other straight line and use this method to control your foot placement.

4. Incorrect Heel-Toe Technique

This problem can be detected by any, or all, of the following:

- You're "goose stepping"—your thigh is coming forward too quickly and the leg is extended before your foot touches on the ground.
- You're walking "flat-footed"—landing with the forward foot flat, instead of landing on the heel.
- You're "lifting" and bouncing.

Here's an exercise that race walkers use to correct the problem:

- Stand upright. Place your left foot forward so that the heel has contact with the ground. Your right foot should be in "lift-off position" so that the toe has contact with the ground. Hold this position and gently shift your body weight back and forth between both legs. This exercise will help to strengthen the muscles and tendons that you use in the heel-toe technique.

What Else?

These are the most common problems seen in beginning speedwalkers. Chances are, if you don't "feel right," you're probably doing one or more of these things. Also be aware of "creeping," bending the back leg too much as it passes under the center of your body. In addition, a short, choppy stride means that you probably aren't swiveling your hips quite enough (concentrate on exercises for hip flexibility). And finally, stop and check to see if your body is straining forward or leaning backward. This is usually best observed by someone else, but if you're bouncing and lifting, it might be caused by improper body position and/or improper foot technique.

As you advance, you'll want to polish your technique more and more. I suggest you walk with other people and occasionally check each other for improper techniques. Remember, however, that variations in style are not indications of problems—they are natural. As you become more experienced, you'll easily be able to tell who is walking incorrectly and who has simply developed an individual style.

VARIETY WALKING

No one expects you to get out there your first day and speedwalk a mile or more. Since you want this to be a sport you stick with, it's important that you make it one you can do *effectively.* That's why I've developed the concept of "variety walking." Based on Swedish runner Gosta Holmer's idea of "speedplay," which consists of a change between slow and fast running, variety walking is intended to keep you moving while you polish your technique and increase your stamina. Here's how it works:

Start out slowly. Speedwalk for about a quarter of a mile, about five city blocks. Check your technique—straight spine, heel-toe, push-pull with locked knees, and a slight hip swivel. Now, change over to regular walking—bend both knees and walk as you usually do. After a few blocks, or a quarter of a mile, change back to speedwalking.

As you progress, naturally your distances will improve. You might want to speedwalk half a mile, then walk regularly for a quarter to half a mile. Later, you can use the Mexican mobile exercises (see pp. 69–75) whenever you want to loosen up or add something different to your routine. Variety walking is successful because it eases the pressure on you. You know you're exercising and moving along, but you aren't pushing yourself beyond your limits. Another wonderful advantage—it minimizes the charley horse many beginners experience.

HOW FAST, HOW FAR?

Although I have been stressing slowness, there comes a time when everyone wants to know, "How fast should I go?" Of course, my answer is always, "As fast as you want to and as fast as you feel the need to." But most people want some facts and figures, so here goes.

I speedwalk a quarter of a mile in three minutes. Beginning students average from four and a half to five minutes. My average speedwalking mile is done in thirteen minutes, while beginners usually finish a mile in sixteen to eighteen minutes.

As you can see, these times are considerably slower than many running times. That's because speedwalking is more controlled and involves more body movement. You'll still be getting a great workout *and* using up lots of calories. As a matter of fact, many walkers are convinced they tone up and slim down faster with this exercise than with any other.

4.
WARMING UP

Warm-ups do a lot of good things for you, but most important, they can help to prevent injury. That's right, a few minutes of stretching and relaxing can minimize the chance that you'll hurt yourself in the process of helping yourself. That's because your body, like the engine of a car, needs to be warmed up for efficient operation. Cold engines can sputter, spit, and stall; cold muscles can strain, sprain, and tear. You can greatly reduce your vulnerability to this type of injury by relaxing and stretching before you begin speedwalking. Warm-ups get your blood circulating, give your muscles, tendons, and ligaments time to become more flexible, and can even improve your performance. In addition, warm-ups give you some "mental time" to prepare yourself, to concentrate on your goals, and to psych up before you begin speedwalking. Remember, exercise is stressful to the body, so it's not only a good idea to warm up before you speedwalk—IT'S ESSENTIAL THAT YOU DO AT LEAST FIVE MINUTES OF WARM-UP EXERCISES BEFORE EACH SPEEDWALKING WORKOUT.

A group of speedwalkers warming up outdoors. *Photo by Truman Moore*

LESS BOUNCE TO THE OUNCE

A warm-up is intended to s-t-r-e-t-c-h the muscles. Stretching does not mean bouncing, bobbing, or jerking. This type of action has the reverse effect—it triggers a reflex action that contracts muscles. Keeping this in mind, go into your stretches slowly and gently. You can begin by holding each stretch to a slow count of ten. As you advance, try to hold each stretch for a count of twenty.

OVERSTRETCHING

When you hold a stretch for a count of ten to twenty, you should feel the tension slowly diminish. If, instead, your discomfort increases, or even turns into real pain, you are probably overstretching. In this case, stretch less and slowly increase the pull with every few warm-up sessions.

DOORWAY WARM-UPS

These warm-ups are created for busy people. They should take only five to fifteen minutes and can be done right in the doorway before you leave your home or apartment and begin speedwalking. Remember, the purpose of a warm-up is to stretch and relax. If you are really tense or "tight," take a few extra minutes and do the special "Weekend Warm-Ups" on pp. 67–69. This is a series of four extra exercises that will help increase your flexibility. Remember, too, that since the doorway warm-ups can be done standing up, you can do them during the day, or anytime you feel like relaxing and warming up tense muscles.

Begin each warm-up session with "The Total Relaxer" (see p. 27).

1.Ankle Seesaw

Raise your left heel off the floor, so that the left foot is "on point." Return the foot to its original position, while simultaneously lifting the right heel off the floor. Keep this up at a fast pace. Do this twenty to thirty times.

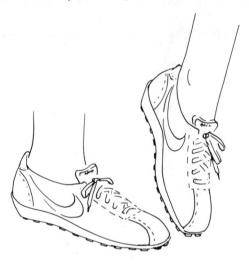

2.In-and-Out Knee Kick.

Stand up straight. Bring your right knee up to your waist. Return the leg to a standing position. Now bring your right knee up and straight out so that it's at a 90 degree angle to your body. Repeat quickly, in a kicking motion, ten times. Do this ten times with each leg. Alternating legs.

3.Bumps and Grinds

Stand up straight. Slowly contract the stomach and buttock muscles simultaneously; just as in the "Pelvic Tilt" on p. 67. Hold—release. Do this at least ten times.

4.Lunge Step

Hold on to a doorknob or the back of a chair. Stretch your right leg back as far as possible, keeping it straight. At the same time

In-and-Out Knee Kick

go into a deep knee bend with your left leg. Make sure to keep your body upright. Hold this position for a slow count of ten (remember not to bounce!). Do this three times with each leg, alternating legs. This exercise must be done *slowly.*

5.Korean Squat

Position your legs so that they are just a little bit more than shoulder width apart. Squat down, trying to get your thighs parallel to the floor. Use your arms to push your legs as far apart as possible. Hold this position for a slow count of ten. You should feel the stretch in the inner thigh area. Do this three times.

6.Hamstring Stretch

Stand with your feet together and your knees straight. Rest your hands on your back. Slowly bend forward, keeping your back straight and your head up. Continue bending forward until you feel a stretch in the back of your legs and knees. Hold this position while taking a deep breath. Slowly resume standing position. Do this three times.

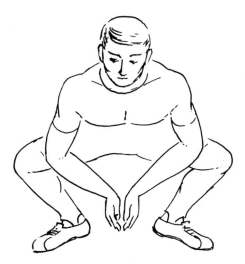

Korean Squat

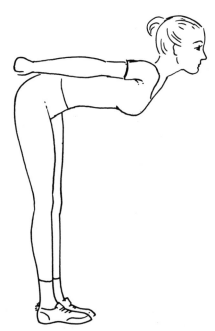

Hamstring Stretch

7. Double and Single Runner's Stretch

Extend your arms at shoulder level. Step back so that your fingertips are about three inches from a wall. Lean forward and place your palms against the wall. Keep your body straight, heels on floor (avoid arching your back), bend your elbows, and lean forward slowly. You should feel a strong pull along the backs of your legs, right down to the Achilles tendons. Hold for a slow count of ten. Do this three times.

Next, lean forward and bend your left leg, resting your left foot behind your right knee. Hold and repeat with the opposite leg. Do this three times with each leg.

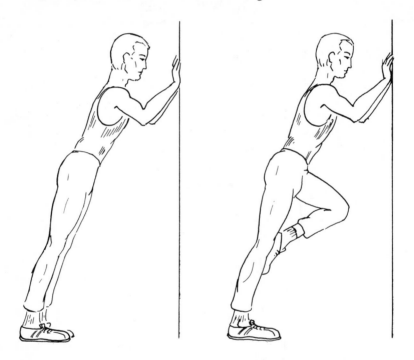

WEEKEND WARM-UPS

These "extra" warm-up exercises are for when you have more time, when you feel you need just a little more relaxation and stretching, or want variety in your regular warm-ups.

1.Pelvic Tilt in Basic Position

This is especially good for lower spine flexibility. Assume the basic position (lie on back, knees bent, feet on the floor, legs comfortably apart). Put your hand, palm down, under the small of your back. Contract your buttock muscles and your lower stomach muscles as hard as you can. Hold to a count of five. You should feel the small of your back press against your hand. Release your muscles. Do this five times.

2.The Cyclist

Lie on your back and bicycle ten to twenty times. Next, try sitting up while you bicycle. If this position proves too difficult, it's an indication that you'll need to strengthen weak stomach muscles. (See "Semi-Sit-Up" and "The Total Sit-Up" on pp. 28 and 34.)

3.Head-to-Toe Stretch

Sit with the soles of your feet together. Grasp your ankles and pull your head toward your feet. Hold, without bouncing, for a slow count of ten to twenty. Sit up and press your knees apart with your elbows—you should feel this in your inner thighs. Hold for a slow count of ten to twenty.

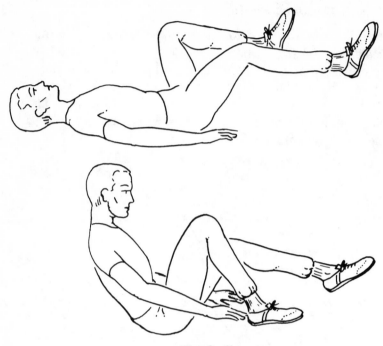

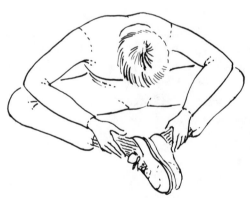

The Cyclist

Head-to-Toe Stretch

4. *Leg Split*

Sit with legs wide apart. Grasp one leg with both hands and gently pull your head down toward your knee. Hold for a count

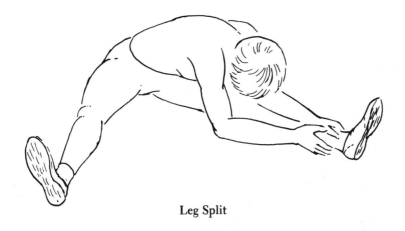

Leg Split

of ten. Repeat this position with the other leg. Hold. Repeat three times with each leg, alternating legs.

THE MEXICAN MOBILE EXERCISES

These are special, unique ways to warm up *as you speedwalk*. These ingenious exercises were developed in Mexico, where race walking is fast becoming a favorite national sport. The Mexican mobile exercises are not only great ways to warm up, you can use them during variety walking, when you're alternating walking with speedwalking. You can combine them on your "off days" with the heel-toe technique. You can do them anytime, anywhere, as a great way to limber up shoulders, arms, and waist. In addition, many speedwalkers like to wind down with the Mexican mobile exercises. They do a few blocks or laps of these "moving stretches" before they begin their cool-down exercises.

These mobile exercises can be done with the heel-toe technique, but when you are learning them, you might want to master the upper body movement before you combine it with the lower body technique. Experiment, and use the method that works best for you. You'll find that mobile exercises are an invigorating way to begin your speedwalking sessions.

WARMING UP WITH MEXICAN MOBILE EXERCISES
Photos by Mel Levine

The "Windmill"

The "Elbow Seesaw"

The "Cradle"

The "Armswing"

1. Windmill Circling

Begin circling your arms in a backward direction only. Keep this up for about twenty strides or more.

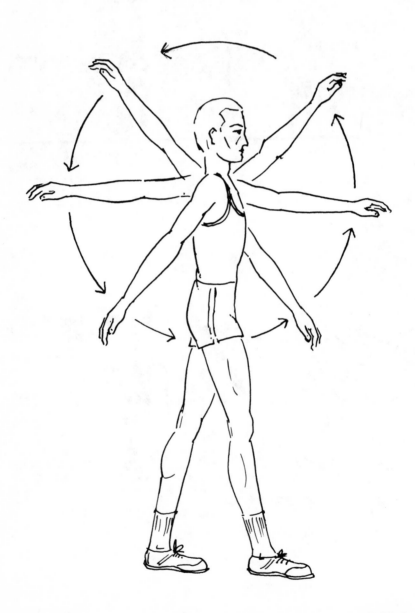

2. Elbow Seesaw

Place your fingertips on the tips of your shoulders. As your right elbow moves upward, your left foot will step forward. This will become a natural countermovement as you practice. Walk this way for about fifty strides.

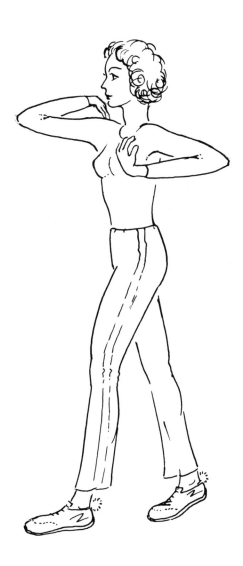

3. The Cradle Swing

Take a step with your right leg as you pull both arms to the right side. Repeat with the left leg and left side. This is a good way to slim your waist, but it may be difficult at first, as it involves a bit more coordination. Cradle swing for about fifty strides.

In order to be most effective, these exercises should be done one after the other, smoothly and without interruption. Remember to keep moving and to add the heel-toe technique as soon as you're able to.

5.
COOLING DOWN

Just as your body needs time to prepare for activity, it also needs time to wind down. If you've ever watched horses at the track, you'll have noticed that after a race they slowly circle the track for a few laps until they are cooled down enough to rest. Stopping exercise suddenly can result in unpleasant side effects: muscle soreness, dizziness, and even cramps. Cooling down means letting your body slowly resume its natural pulse rate and temperature.

The first few cool-downs I describe can be done at the track, on the street, or wherever you speedwalk. The subsequent ones involve more stretching and should be done sitting or lying, so you'll probably want to wait until you get home to do these. Remember, cooling down should be _done gradually_; it should be _relaxing_; and it should be done _after every vigorous speedwalking workout._

MOVING INTO YOUR COOL-DOWNS

Cooling off should begin while you're still out there and moving. Here's how to prepare your body gently for the end of a vigorous speedwalk.

- Gradually reduce your walking speed.
- You may want to do one or more of the Mexican mobile exercises as you walk more slowly.
- When you have significantly reduced your speed and have hit a regular walking pace, stop and begin the following cool-downs.

1.Rag Doll Pendulum

Let your body hang loosely from your hips. Keeping your legs a bit more than shoulder width apart, swing gently from one leg to the other. Swing three times from the right leg to the left. Then grasp the right leg and press your head as close as possible to the leg. Release the leg and swing three times from side to side. Now hold the left leg and press your head close to the leg. You will feel the stretch in the back of each leg.

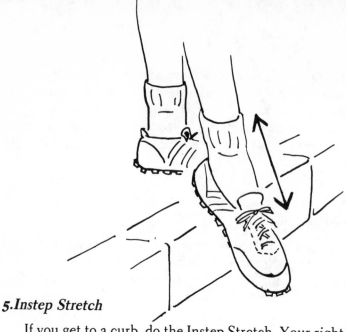

5.Instep Stretch

If you get to a curb, do the Instep Stretch. Your right heel rests on the curb. Press downward with your toes, so you feel your instep s-t-r-e-t-c-h-i-n-g. Hold to count of ten. Do this three times with each foot, alternating.

3.Crisscross Stretch

Cross your right foot over your left foot. Your right leg should be bent at the knee, while your left leg remains straight. Slowly bend forward, reaching down as far as you can. Hold for a

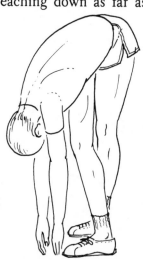

count of twenty. Do this three times with each leg, alternating legs.

4. The Stork

Grasp your right ankle with your right hand so that your right foot is behind your back. Hold on to a lamppost, tree, or anything sturdy with your left hand. Gently pull your foot back and up until you feel the stretch in the front of your thigh.

For a more advanced version; lean forward until your body is almost parallel to the ground.

2.Runner's Stretch

See p. 66.

AT-HOME COOL-DOWNS

1.Shin Stretcher

Sit back on your heels, feet extended. Hold this position for one to two minutes.

2. The Cat

Start on your hands and knees, head up, back flat. Slowly lower your head as you hunch your back. Slowly raise your head as you lower your back. Do this three times.

3. The A Frame

Begin on your hands and knees, just as you did for "The Cat." Your toes should be curled under. Straighten your knees and press your heels toward the floor. Hold for a count of ten to twenty.

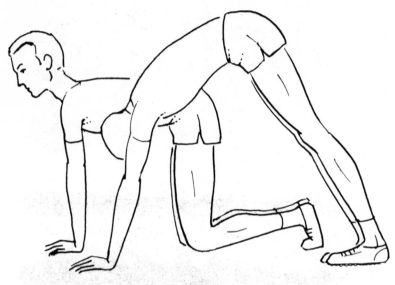

The A Frame

The Windshield Wiper

4. The Cliff Hanger

Lie on your back. Slowly bring both legs overhead and support your lower back with your hands. (for more on this technique, refer to "The High Roller" on p. 28). Once your legs are overhead, relax your knees so that they bend slightly and the legs are hanging by their own weight. Breathe in and out deeply. Hold for a slow count of ten.

5. The Windshield Wiper

As you get more advanced, try straightening your legs out and swinging them slowly from side to side while supporting your lower back with your hands.

A RELAXING FINISH

Once you've finished these gentle stretching cool-downs, you might want to try the "Head-to-Toe Stretch" (see p. 33) and the "Leg Split" (see pp. 67–69). Before you go back to your daily activities, take a few moments to do your "Total Relaxer" (see p. 27). At this point, you should be cooled off, stretched out, and very relaxed.

6.

ENCOURAGEMENT

Exercise doesn't only involve muscles, strength, and flexibility—it's also about attitude and motivation. If you've tried other exercise programs and discontinued them, or if you've never tried any, this chapter is as important to you as those that preceded it. The subject of this chapter is how you can encourage yourself to stay with the program, and how you can make speedwalking an activity tailored to your own special needs and goals.

I think speedwalking is the best exercise there is. You will too. But knowing that an exercise is good for you, and even realizing that it can be fun, noncompetitive, and easy, won't keep you at it. There are times in everyone's life when it just seems necessary to "take a day off." Sometimes that day turns into a week, that week into a month, and so on, until you realize that it's been a very long time since your last workout. Of course, if you're ill it often becomes unavoidable to take time off from vigorous exercise.

Then comes the "exercise block." You're afraid to get out there and pick up where you left off because you've gotten out of shape, lost your enthusiasm, and most of all, you feel as if you've failed. Well, take it from me, *quitting does not equal failing*. We all feel like quitting once in a while. And for some of us, a day off, or even a few days off, can be helpful.

How do you get back in the routine after you've taken a brief exercise "holiday"? When should you take time off from speedwalking? And most important, how do you get the discipline and the determination to keep it up? These are important questions. To be successful at any activity, you'll need practical answers and solutions that really *work*!

PERSONAL GOALS=PERSONAL SUCCESS

Everyone wants to be fit, slim, and healthy. I believe that these goals are within just about everyone's reach. Not all people can reach these goals at the same rate, however, or in the same manner. That's why it's so important to tailor your goals to fit your body, your mind, and your life. Charts that measure progress and tell you what you *should* weigh, how fast you *should* move, and how much exercise you *should* be getting are fine if the person who made those charts knows you personally. The chances are, though, that those charts are referring to the "average person."

The trouble is, no one is really "average." We're all special in some important way. Take our needs to work out a set number of times per week. Although I've been involved in exercise and sports for twenty-five years, there are plenty of times when I've needed a few days off, days to relax, read a book, sit in the sun, or just to rest and feel lazy. I don't feel guilty about these days, and I don't think of them as "nonproductive." I *need* these times to gather my energy and rebuild my enthusiasm. The chances are, if you've been involved in sports or exercise for several years, you feel the same way too. Even the most dedicated athletes often "break training" and let loose once in a while.

If you've never really been involved in a regular program of exercise, you're probably not accustomed to your own rhythms. It's easy to set lofty goals on paper, goals like attaining certain speeds or distances or finally taking off those extra fifteen pounds. Goals are important to an exercise program, but unrealistic goals can defeat even the most well-intentioned, well-planned program. What are realistic goals? That depends upon you—your physical condition, your schedule, and of course, your motivation.

Here's an example of how unrealistic goals can result in failure. My student Jane began speedwalking to lose fifteen pounds. She had it all figured out. She'd walk every day for an hour, taking off only on Sunday. To help her reach her goal, she also went on a zero carbohydrate diet (without informing me). After seven days of this program, Jane did lose three pounds, but she also lost her energy. She felt tired and weak and she missed two days at the office. But worst of all, Jane lost her enthusiasm for exercising and thought she just "couldn't cut it." She felt like a quitter. As she explained it: "I tried, I really tried to keep up with the speedwalking. I don't know what happened. It was just too hard for me. I feel like such a softie. I knew I could never be one of those 'fitness buffs.'"

Jane was right about one thing—her speedwalking program was too hard. She hadn't been active since she was in junior high school. As a working woman in her mid-thirties, Jane expected that she could simply don a pair of sneakers and pick up where she left off. But the body doesn't work that way. Speedwalking six hours a week can be vigorous exercise. Such a program must be worked up to. Sometimes this can take as little as a week, but for some people it may take months. Jane didn't give herself a chance. On top of all this, she went on a diet that restricted the very food she needed for fuel. The result—her body weakened and so did her determination. If Jane had taken the time to set realistic goals—ones tailored to her individual needs, she'd still be speedwalking today. And chances are, if she had gone on a healthy diet, she'd also be fifteen pounds lighter. How do you set realistic goals for yourself? Here are some questions you'll need to answer before you set up your exercise program.

1. When was the last time you were involved in a program of regular and vigorous exercise?

2. How active have you been for the past five years?

3. How often will you actually be able to exercise?

4. What are some realistic goals that you can accomplish in the next six months?

5. How can you help yourself, and enlist others to help you to keep up with this exercise program?

MUSCLE USE VERSUS MUSCLE ABUSE

Questions 1 and 2 seem easy enough to answer, but most people have difficulty with them. Why? Because they aren't really sure if what they've been doing is "exercise" or everyday activity. In short, they simply don't know the difference between *muscle use and muscle abuse.*

For example, one woman I know insists that she "doesn't need any more exercise" because she "exercises all day long." This woman has three small children and a large house to take care of. She spends most of her day carrying the baby, running up the stairs, and driving the two older children to day-care and elementary school. It's a hectic schedule. But instead of using her muscles in a well-balanced program that promotes strength and flexibility, she has been abusing them. She's been using the same muscles over and over again while neglecting the rest. A quick check with the speedwalker's strength and flexibility test proved that this very busy woman was inflexible in the hip and shoulder areas, and her stomach muscles needed considerable toning.

Similarly, many business men and women spend a few hours a week or a month, playing tennis or raquetball, and so consider themselves "active." But unlike speedwalking, racket sports don't exercise your entire body. They stress certain muscles and often build up one side of the body more than the other.

How active you've *really* been will be reflected in how flexible you are and in how much stamina you have. If you're not sure if your weekly tennis game or your five block walk to work should be considered well-balanced exercise, take a second look at the results of your speedwalker's strength and flexibility test, or try to do all the exercises in the get-ready program. This will give you a good indication of whether or not you've been using or abusing your muscles.

A word of caution to "seasonal athletes": If your only exercise is skiing during the winter months, or swimming during the summer, you'll need to find a supplementary exercise that can be done year round, one that will keep your muscles toned and flexible. Speedwalking will do this and it will prevent that awful "out of shape" feeling that seasonal athletes constantly complain about.

HOW OFTEN SHOULD YOU SPEEDWALK?

Of course, when we talk about realistic schedules, we must consider how often exercise is practical for *you*. To be effective, speedwalking must be done on a regular basis. Regular, for beginners, means *at least* three times a week. As you progress, you should expand your exercise program to four or five times a week. No matter how enthusiastic you get, however, I suggest you always give your body (and spirit) at least one day off a week.

Although the length of each speedwalking workout will vary according to the shape you're in (beginners, for example, may not be able to sustain more than twenty minutes of intense movement), a good rule of thumb is to aim for a forty-five-minute workout, but remember, this includes about fifteen minutes or more of warm-ups and cool-downs. The workout may also include alternating speedwalking with regular walking or with the Mexican mobile exercises.

SCHEDULES THAT REALLY WORK

Everyone's schedule is different. It's normally assumed that the whole world works from nine to five, or not at all. This assumption has led to many exercise dropouts. Even if you do work a full day, five days a week, chances are that your hours are not strictly nine to five. There are many people who work different hours, vary their shifts, or have the flexibility to set up their own schedules.

Aside from your work schedule, you also have another time-table to consider—your own biological rhythms. These rhythms determine who's out speedwalking first thing in the morning, who prefers to exercise late at night, and who feels that it's essential to exercise in the afternoon. Don't box yourself into a schedule that doesn't coincide with your own rhythms. This can set you up for failure.

Mark Lucas, a fifty-year-old insurance salesman, explains how ignoring his biological timetable almost destroyed his well-planned, well-intentioned speedwalking program:

"I figured the whole thing out on paper. My doctor warned me that at my age I had better start exercising. He suggested brisk walking or jogging. When I heard about speedwalking, I called him immediately. He was enthusiastic and said it sounded like the perfect solution.

"The trouble was that I had tried exercise before and had dropped out when pressures at work forced me to skip sessions. This time I was determined to avoid the problem. I made up my mind that, as much as I hated it, I would get up at seven o'clock every morning and speedwalk for forty-five minutes. This way I'd have my warm-ups, cool-downs, and speedwalking all finished by eight o'clock.

"I soon discovered why I had never exercised that early in the day. I'm just not a morning person. I was so stiff and tight that I wound up doing a whole bunch of extra warm-ups just to be able to feel loose. My speedwalking times were pretty disappointing and I just couldn't summon the enthusiasm to walk over half a mile. I probably would have given up altogether had it not been for a bit of friendly curiosity.

"My neighbor saw me speedwalking and asked for a demonstration. I set it up for the next day and moved my own exercise session to the evening. I couldn't believe the difference! My whole body was much more responsive. I was more flexible, more relaxed, and I walked faster and further. This made it clear—I was an 'evening speedwalker.'

"Now I suddenly find that I *do* have the time in the evening. Between coming home from the office and eating dinner, there's time that I had reserved for "relaxing." Now, I find it is more relaxing to put on my running shoes, do a few warm-ups, speedwalk for a mile, cool down, and join my family for dinner. And there's an extra bonus to this new plan—my son has joined me. He also hated the idea of exercising so early in the morning.

"I figure that if I hadn't realized the importance of my own 'inner timetable,' I'd still be forcing myself to conform to a schedule that just wasn't suited to my special needs."

Are you a morning person or an evening person? To find out when you're at your speedwalking best, try alternating times for two weeks. The first week, speedwalk in the morning, the second in the afternoon or evening. Like Mark, you will probably notice a dramatic difference in your body's response.

MAKE-UPS

Whether you decide to speedwalk in the morning, afternoon, or evening, you should leave some time so you can make up missed sessions. A rigid schedule in which, for example, you only speed-walk at lunch five days a week can work fine—until you have a business meeting, a dentist appointment, or an important errand to take care of. When this happens, you miss your speedwalking for the day. Missing one session isn't the end of the world, but it can signal the end of your discipline and commitment. It's important, especially in the early stages of your program, to try to discipline yourself and stick with it. Later on, when you've gotten into the momentum of regular exercise, you'll find that you can take these annoying interruptions in your stride. Nevertheless, if your schedule is rigid, and you can't find the time to make up these missed sessions, you will find that they can slow you down, and put you farther away from your goals.

How can you makeup missed sessions? Easily. First, when

you set up your exercise schedule, take into consideration that unplanned events happen to everyone. Then set aside alternate times two or three days a week for supplementary or make-up speedwalking sessions. Figure out when you can squeeze in an extra forty-five minutes or so during the week. You may rarely use these times, but it's a good feeling to know that should you need them, they're available. That's what I mean by a schedule that really works!

In addition, you may find, as I have, that alternating exercise times can add a little extra variety to your program. And, another advantage to "banking" these extra sessions is that it gives you the room to expand your speedwalking program. As you progress, you'll probably want to work out more and more.

What should you do if illness, bad weather, or other complications prevent you from speedwalking for a week or more? Obviously you can't add a supplementary week to your calendar, but you can keep your muscles flexible and toned by practicing your get-ready exercises at home every day. You won't be speedwalking, but you *will* be shaping up the muscles you use in speedwalking. You'll still be toning and slimming your body while you uplift your morale and sagging spirits.

What if you don't always have a free forty-five minute block three times a week? Don't eliminate all speedwalking just because you may not have this time all at once. Practice the heel-toe technique on your way to work, limber up in your office, and get in about twenty minutes of speedwalking when you can. One man I know plans a complete forty-five minute walk three times a week, and the other three days he alternates the Mexican mobile exercises with the heel-toe technique on his way to work. Other people prefer to do the get-ready program on their lunch hour three times a week and speedwalk the other times. Find a balance that works for you. Beginning with a program of three workouts a week will give you a basic self-improvement formula. Supplementary workouts are fine, but you should aim for regularly scheduled sessions that gradually increase in intensity and duration. And don't forget variety! Why not try different warm-ups (like some of the weekend warm-ups) or walking in different places? Almost any surface is fine for speedwalking, so vary your walks to include parks, tracks, and city streets. It will provide you with a welcome change of scenery!

What about those times in your life when some special event, such as the Christmas holidays, a long trip, or a wedding, temporarily interrupts your exercise schedule? No one's life is without these interruptions. That's when it is important to remember that exercise, even if it's done only once a week, is never wasted. If you've been working out on a regular basis, and now for a short time can only speedwalk once a week, make sure you don't eliminate that session. It's essential that you keep in touch with the feeling of well-being you get from regular speedwalking. Even if you can only exercise once or twice a week, your body will remember how it feels to be flexible, toned, and energetic—and you will too!

Once you can return to your normal schedule, you'll find that you haven't fallen "hopelessly behind." A simple maintenance schedule during busy weeks can prevent you from being discouraged when it's time to resume your regular activity.

No matter when, where, or how often you work out, always remember to warm up and cool down and to wear running shoes when you speedwalk for any length of time (for more about running shoes, see 103–104). It's fine to speedwalk to the office in low-heeled, sensible shoes, but for more intense workouts, running shoes will protect you from injury and allow the maximum freedom of movement. In addition, if you've planned a "mini-workout" at lunchtime or any other point in the day, be sure you're prepared—wear clothes that are loose and comfortable, without restricting waistbands, belts, or elastic. One friend of mine always keeps an extra pair of sweat pants and running shoes in her office. This way, if she has the time, she can partake in a spontaneous speedwalking session. A little bit of experimentation on your part, will provide a whole variety of easy and sensible solutions to the problems of scheduling regular exercise sessions.

MOTIVATION

Motivation is the key ingredient in every successful exercise program. To be successful, you have to want to succeed. Although this sounds obvious, many people set themselves up for failure. They make unrealistic demands on their bodies and on their time. Once you've found your own rhythm, set up a realistic schedule, and decided what you want to accomplish in terms of your own needs and abilities, you'll still need that special extra—motivation. For this very reason I don't like to think of speedwalking as just a physical exercise—it should be a *whole person exercise*. Involving your whole person, your mind as well as your body, will give you that extra "edge."

One way to build motivation is to rethink some of your old ideas about exercise. Speedwalking should *not* be grueling torture. It does *not* have to be competitive and you should *never* use it as "punishment" for eating a piece of chocolate cake or for not exercising for two weeks. If you associate exercise with pain and punishment, naturally it will be something you'll want to avoid doing. Think of speedwalking as pleasure, as a reward for a hard day's work, as something you deserve because you really want to look better and feel better.

Perhaps it sounds unimportant, but discarding some of the old, defeatist attitudes you may have had about exercise can make big changes in your motivation and your discipline. To help you develop this motivation, here's a "mental exercise" devised by my coauthor. It really helps!

Find a quiet place where you can be alone without interruption. Close your eyes and in your mind's eye picture yourself speedwalking. See yourself moving along at a steady and rhythmic pace. Watch as your muscles flex and contract. See your hips moving and your arms gently swinging. Try to feel the exhilarating power of your own body. Take this image through to its completion. Visualize yourself cooling down, changing clothes, and looking in the mirror. You look slimmer, your body is more toned, stronger and healthier. You feel great.

Concentrate on all the energy in your body. Retain this positive image of yourself. Fix it in your mind.

When you open your eyes, remember this healthy, powerful picture of yourself. Keep it with you as you speedwalk and repeat this same "mind picture" before you warm up or anytime you feel like quitting. A positive self-image will help you to stay with a speedwalking program that can improve your health and your looks. Substitute this image of yourself for all those old, loser ones you may have. Don't use exercise as a torturous way to reduce from a size 12 to a size 8, or as a way to "atone" for a night of drinking or overeating.

New York/New Jersey psychotherapist Alan Schneider puts it this way: "You can use speedwalking as a method of getting to know yourself. It's a sport that allows you to figure out your own rhythms while you increase your ability. Forget judgments, competitions, and unrealistic goals. Learn to develop motivation and self-confidence as well as technique and speed. Once you've accomplished this, you've accomplished more than an effective exercise program—you've learned to accept yourself."

TO COMPETE OR NOT TO COMPETE

Many people need to be motivated by the thrill of victory. Others can be discouraged simply by the possibility of defeat. If competition adds to your motivation and improves your performance, speedwalk with a few friends, time yourself, and hold a weekly race meeting. If you decide to compete with others, however, don't overload the odds by walking against people who are much older or younger, or more or less fit than you are. Another thing to consider is height. Longer legs usually mean longer strides and faster times. If you're five foot five and racing with someone who is six foot two, chances are you'll be the loser simply because your stride is shorter. Instead of competing, you might find that you prefer speedwalking with someone who can pace you, and encourage you to keep going and improve your own time.

If competition makes you anxious, rather than enthusiastic, it's best not to compare yourself to anyone else. Set your own goals in terms of time and distance. If you need to measure yourself against someone else, check back to p. 58, where I've listed some of the average times for beginning and intermediate speedwalkers.

MEASURING YOUR PROGRESS

The most effective way to increase motivation is to see real progress. The trouble is that many people simply don't know how to assess their own achievement. Charts and scales are one way to measure advancement, but they're not the only way. One woman I know found her own personal method of measuring improvement. Here's how she explains it:

"My goals were to keep up with a daily speedwalking routine, complete with warm-ups and cool-downs, and to promote more flexibility in the hip area (I didn't do so well on the speedwalker's strength and flexibility test). In addition, I wanted to take off an extra ten pounds—weight I had put on after my last child was born over twelve years ago. I began in the usual way; I weighed myself every day. But I discovered that if I didn't lose weight right away, I'd get discouraged and feel like quitting. I soon realized that daily weigh-ins were out for me. They were counterproductive because they didn't help me with my motivation and discipline. I also found that if I timed myself while I walked I got nervous and anxious. This sort of constant 'testing' made me feel pressured to succeed.

"Every time I began to walk I thought to myself, 'If I can't walk at least half a mile in such and such a time, this proves that I am hopeless, out of shape, etc.' Since I already knew I wasn't a great athlete, these negative thoughts certainly didn't encourage me. That's when I decided that if I was to keep up with speedwalking, I had better find new and personal ways to measure the progress I was making

"Instead of standing on the scale, I stood in front of the mirror. It was easier to notice changes in my figure (like an immediate firming up of my flabby arms) than it was to calculate lost pounds. I also tried on a pair of slacks that had always been tight around the waist. After three weeks I could see that they were beginning to loosen up. Instead of timing myself, I just tried to increase my speedwalking workouts by ten minutes each week. I figured that walking longer meant that I wouldn't be sacrificing form for speed. This method helped me to check my technique as I moved, instead of forcing me to check my stopwatch every other second. As for distance, instead of counting miles, I counted telephone poles. This made walking fun, not a mathematical problem. I was never one for calculating distance, speed, and pulse rates. I developed my own special measurements, because I'm different from anyone else. Those charts may work for the 'average person' but they have never worked for me.

"The result—after six months I'm speedwalking four hours a week and I've doubled my distance. I can't tell exactly how much weight I've lost, but my clothes fit me perfectly, and those formerly 'inflexible hips' have improved too. I can now do every exercise in the speedwalker's strength and flexibility test, *and* all the advanced exercises in the get-ready program."

If you're not "one for charts, tables, and measurements," why not try some of these methods?

1. Check yourself in the mirror, instead of weighing in.

2. Use familiar landmarks as goals instead of setting goals in miles.

3. Increase your total exercise time five to ten minutes each week instead of timing yourself with a stopwatch. Your speed *will* increase naturally.

4. Refer back to the speedwalker's strength and flexibility test to see how you've improved in specific areas.

If, however, you don't get discouraged by charts, scales, or stopwatches, here's a good way to record your progress. Keep a chart that notes your speedwalking times and distances, and the improvements in flexibility and/or weight loss. Keep this chart in a place where you'll see it before you begin your daily workout—the closet where you keep your running shoes, beside the door where you do your warm-ups, or for real encouragement, beside your mirror! This way you'll "psych yourself up" just before you begin each walk.

BUILDING DISCIPLINE

When I tell people what I do for a living, the usual question is, "How do you get the discipline to exercise regularly?" The answer is that I work on it. No one is born disciplined, it's something we all must develop. For me discipline and motivation go hand in hand. Once I see progress, I am motivated to stick with it, but of course that progress can never come about without a bit of self-discipline. I don't believe anyone is "hopeless" and can't conform to a routine that is sensible and practical. But some people *do* have more trouble with self-discipline than others. That's why I've decided to include some methods that have worked for me and for my coauthor.

We don't believe that self-discipline is a result of self-punishment. Don't threaten yourself into exercising regularly—encourage yourself. You don't really need an "iron will" to get into a speedwalking routine—that's because this is a sport that's easy and natural. But you *will* need to exert some self-control when you feel like dropping out or missing a few sessions too many. As I've said before, everyone feels like cutting out a workout once in a while. If you need the time to rest and gather energy, or to rethink your goals, that's okay, but I'm sure you know the difference between a well-deserved break and "playing hooky." And sometimes you can accomplish your goals "with a little help from your friends."

ONE STEP AT A TIME

It's a day when you feel like crawling right back into bed. You're tired, discouraged, and maybe you're bothered with problems at work or at home. You feel like sleeping, eating—anything but exercising. These "blah" days can pose real obstacles to self-discipline. At these times, the thought of a vigorous speedwalking session can simply seem impossible and overwhelming.

In reality, exercise, especially outdoor exercise, is the best cure for the "blahs" that I know of. The tough thing is getting out there and realizing this for yourself. Here's a method that can work for you: Instead of letting yourself become overwhelmed and immobilized by the thought of a lengthy speedwalk, take it one small step at a time. Rather than crawling back into bed (or wherever you go to escape), begin by doing just "The Total Relaxer" on p. 27. This is a terrific way to calm yourself. Next step? Try the three-stage relaxing formula on pp. 125–26. Once you've gotten this far, you'll begin to feel a bit better.

Now begin a slow, gentle warm-up routine. Don't even think about speedwalking yet. Just promise yourself that you'll take it one small step at a time. When you've finished warming up, if you still can't seem to force yourself into speedwalking—well, at least you'll have done some exercise for the day.

Chances are if you take it slowly and easily you'll notice two important things have happened—one, you *feel* better, and two, you'll *want to try speedwalking.* You may not have a long or particularly vigorous workout (although many people find that what begins as a "blah" day can turn into a successful, energetic one), but you will have begun to exert some self-control and self-discipline. And that's the secret to building discipline. Not all at once, not forced or threatened—but gently, one step at a time. Try it!

THE SPEEDWALKER'S SUPPORT SYSTEM

Many things are best accomplished in groups. Sometimes "two heads are better than one." In the case of speedwalking, it may be that two wills are stronger than one. On days when it seems far easier to skip your exercise, calling a few friends to cancel may force you to reconsider. That's why the "buddy method" works.

A support system can help you in many ways. Friends can offer you encouragement. They can also check your form, time your walks, and keep you going when you feel like quitting. Just knowing that someone else shares your occasional "lapses" in discipline, makes your own needs and rhythms easier to accept—and to deal with. Remember, though, a support system should not be a competitive arrangement. It should be one of cooperation and group motivation—and it should also be fun!

You can set up a group yourself by asking friends, neighbors, or family members. You can meet new people simply by speedwalking in public parks and streets—people will probably come up to you and ask you more about what you're doing. The nice thing about speedwalking is that it's "do-able" by just about everyone. So ask those sedentary friends to give up a lunch date and join you for a quick walk—soon you'll have a network of people who can encourage you to keep going and to keep improving!

7.

SPECIAL NEEDS

We're all different—and we're all special. That's why every new speedwalker has some questions and problems that need to be discussed. In this chapter we try to answer a few common, and a few not-so-common questions. What should you wear? What should you eat? What about your feet, your schedule, and your age? When I conduct speedwalking clinics, men and women ask me these questions again and again. They're concerned about problems they feel no one else shares. They're worried they'll make a "mistake," eat the wrong foods, or injure themselves in some way. Many speedwalkers are running dropouts. They ask me about "carbohydrate loading," overtraining, shin splints, and heel spurs. Other speedwalkers are new to a regular exercise program. They wonder how they'll be able to walk in cold or excessively warm weather. They're worried about exercise during menstruation or old age. Many of the answers I give them are based on my own experience; for others, I've turned to nutritionists, doctors, and specialists in sports medicine.

Although not all medical authorities agree on questions of diet, or methods of training, they all concede that *sensible* exercise and *sensible* diet improve health and give participants a general feeling of well-being. And so the word *sensible* has become my guideline for a successful exercise program. You won't find any "quickie" cures or fad diets in this chapter, not only because they're not sensible, but because THEY DON'T WORK. Walking five miles a day, losing six pounds a week, and eating only protein may sound terrific, but are they effective methods for you? In this chapter we'll explore questions like these, and give you practical, sound, and *sensible* answers.

WHAT SHOULD I WEAR?

I've seen people working out, running in the park, and attending exercise class in designer jogging suits, glitter socks, and radio headsets. There's nothing wrong with wanting to look chic while you exercise, but I'd suggest you wait until you've developed your routine and mastered your technique before you become a candidate for the athletic "best-dressed list."

Basically, what you wear for speedwalking depends upon when and where you'll be exercising. If you're simply "heel-toeing" it to the office, you won't need to dress as you would for a full forty-five-minute walk. And of course, in warm and cold weather your clothing will differ.

To simplify things, I've devised what I like to call "the basic speedwalker's uniform." This is what you'd wear for a full workout in mild weather. It will be your first layer in winter, and it's the uniform you should store in your office, school, or gym if you intend to speedwalk during the day.

THE BASIC SPEEDWALKER'S UNIFORM

1. *Avoid tight elastic bands on wrists, ankles, and waist.* These can cause chafing and blisters, and can hamper circulation. In addition, a tight waistband of any kind can contribute to the discomfort of the "dreaded stitch."

2. *Choose a 100 percent cotton tee shirt since they absorb perspiration best.* Many of my students prefer to wear a shirt in a slightly larger size than they ordinarily would. That's because the movement involved in speedwalking (torso and arms, especially) can result in your too-tight tee shirt riding up, twisting around your middle, or more embarrassingly, splitting along arm and shoulder seams. If your present tee shirts are too body-conforming, you might try this very practical solution.

3. *Wear Socks.* Cotton is usually preferred for absorbancy. Some people like wool, but make sure you choose a natural fiber that lets your hot feet breathe. Athletic socks come in all varieties, lengths, and styles. Long tube socks are great for winter, and short anklets are ideal for hot summer days. The purpose of wearing socks is to protect your feet from painful blisters, to provide a cushion, and to absorb perspiration. For this reason, your socks must fit properly and should be discarded if they bunch up or fold while you're walking. A lumpy seam can rub against a toe and cause blistering and sores. Always wear clean socks—dirty ones can contribute to blisters and athlete's foot. Remember to choose socks carefully and examine them regularly for damage, worn spots, and overly tight or sagging elastic tops.

4. *Underwear—wear it!* Even in warm weather. It absorbs perspiration, gives you support, and prevents embarrassing incidents. I have one friend who "fell out" of his short nylon running shorts and became the talk of the speedwalking clinic! Men usually prefer to wear a cotton athletic supporter, or Jockey shorts. Women should avoid nylon underpants and wear comfortable cotton ones with elastic that doesn't bind (especially around the thighs). Most women prefer to wear a bra for comfort and support. Underwear manufacturers are finally catering to the athletic woman by creating bras for sports. Try some of these, they are generally soft, supportive, and nonirritating (especially on the shoulders). If you are fairly large-breasted, make sure your bra gives you the support you need to prevent uncomfortable bouncing, but try to stay away from underwires that dig into your ribs as you move your torso.

5. *Shorts.* They should be loose-fitting, buttonless, beltless, and zipperless. Preferably, they should have a slightly flared leg, so they don't rub or chafe. Cotton or nylon are both good

choices as long as the waistband doesn't pinch or chafe. If you're a bit overweight and reluctant to don shorts right away, try loose-fitting sweat pants. These have drawstring waists and are now made in a variety of lighter, more fashionable fabrics than the traditional gray sweat suit material. If your legs chafe when they come in contact with each other, or rub against your shorts, try a light coating of Vaseline on your inner thighs; this will eliminate discomfort and prevent the accompanying rash.

RUNNING SHOES

They used to be called "sneakers," but now that everyone is taking athletics more seriously, running shoes have become serious business. I must admit that I had not always been so concerned about the type of running shoes I wore. I bought an inexpensive pair and wound up with blisters, and aches and pains in my feet, ankles, and thighs. So running shoes are important, and choosing them carefully can't be emphasized enough.

Runners are traditionally more concerned about footwear than most athletes. That's because they're pounding away at their feet and legs with more than three times their body weight. As a speedwalker, you won't be subjecting your feet and leg muscles to this kind of wear and tear, but you do need to pay careful attention to the type of shoe you purchase.

First, it should fit! Although this sounds obvious, many men and women show up for my clinics in borrowed running shoes, torn sneakers, and even Wedgies! Women should buy shoes made for women's feet. Shoes in a corresponding men's size are often too wide for most female feet.

Choose a "light" shoe. Runners often require a shoe with heavy cushioning, but since you won't be pounding the pavement, you can wear a lighter shoe that's less cumbersome and probably less expensive. Make sure the shoe is flexible. Hold it in your hand and bend it. Imitate the heel-toe movement you'll be doing when you speedwalk. If the shoe doesn't "give" easily, try another. Flexibility is of the utmost importance for speedwalkers. Resiliency is another factor you should check for. When you press the sole of the shoe, it should feel like a sponge, rather than like a heavy, nonspringy surface.

In addition to flexibility and resiliency, the running shoe should have ample toe room. Pointed or squared-off fronts can cause your toes to rub against the tip of the shoe. This results in sores, calluses, or blood blisters under the toenail (black toenail).

When purchasing running shoes, I suggest you go to a specialty store. Avoid large department stores or discount shoe stores that sell "running type" shoes at suspiciously low prices (often these are only imitations of the real thing). Athletic or sporting goods stores are usually staffed by experienced walkers and runners. Explain that you'll be speedwalking, not running, and need a lightweight, flexible, and resilient shoe. Try on several. Don't leave the store with a shoe that needs to be "broken in." You'll wind up breaking your spirit and your stride, instead of the shoe. Of course, some shoes do take a bit of getting used to. But this process shouldn't result in blisters, sores, or aching feet.

EVERYDAY SHOES FOR MINI-SPEEDWALKS

If you decide to speedwalk to the bus, the supermarket, or a few blocks to work, it isn't always practical to change into running shoes. In this case you can wear everyday shoes, depending of course on how well they fit, and what you call "everyday." For men, narrow lasts and raised heels, and for women high heels, spikes, or Wedgies are absolutely dangerous. High heels shorten the Achilles tendon, place all your weight on the ball of your foot, and slant your body at an unnatural angle. They also can cause sprained or broken ankles, can be a major cause of back strain, and are generally inflexible. If that isn't enough, consider this: They can cause serious accidents on icy pavements, get caught in tiny cracks and openings, and prevent you from moving quickly and eas-

BAD   BETTER   BEST

ily. Obviously when I talk about everyday shoes, I mean shoes with low-heeled crepe or rubber soles that fit comfortably and are fairly flexible. Laced shoes are better and more supportive than slip-ons or loafers. You don't have to wear absolutely flat shoes, but stay away from anything that lifts your heel much higher than the ball of your foot.

In addition, if you've been wearing high heels on a daily basis, you'll need to get used to running shoes or low heels gradually. Many women complain that after wearing high heels they feel dizzy or uncomfortable and experience aches in their legs when they switch to lower heels. This is because they've become too accustomed to one heel height and their muscles have strained and atrophied to accommodate fashion. To remedy this situation, try the foot strengthening exercises on p. 123. In addition, wear running shoes around the house and on weekends. Buy moderate heels and switch shoes as often as possible. I know spike heels look terrific with evening wear, so enjoy them—but alternate with medium heels and running shoes as often as possible.

HOW TO CHOOSE EVERYDAY SHOES

Are those two-inch heels really okay? Do your cordovan oxfords qualify for speedwalks to work and back? Here are some important tips that will help you decide which shoes really fit, before you wear the wrong ones and suffer with corns, calluses, and aching feet.

1. *When you buy new shoes, don't purchase them in the morning.* Your feet swell during the course of the day, and the

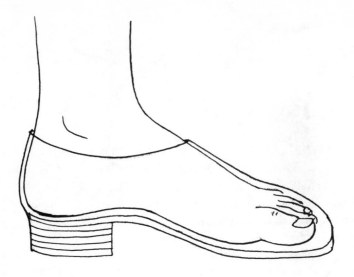

shoes should fit comfortably at the end of the day, when your feet are a bit larger.

2. *Don't buy shoes of plastic or other man-made materials.* Leather and fabric shoes breathe more easily. In other words, they don't trap your feet in little sauna baths that can cause infections, blisters, athlete's foot, and unpleasant odors.

3. *Never buy shoes, or speedwalk in shoes, that need to be "broken in."* If the shoe fits, it should feel comfortable in the store. Don't attempt to recycle a pair of sensible-looking oxfords that never really felt comfortable. If they hurt now, they'll be killing you later!

4. *Don't buy size, buy fit.* One manufacturer's size 8 may be another's size 7. When buying shoes, leave your vanity at home and choose a larger size if you need it.

5. *To test for proper fit, the end of your longest toe should be a thumb's width away from the end of the shoe while you are standing.* You should have enough room across the widest part to be able to pinch the leather or fabric. When you stand barefoot, compare the width of your foot to the width of your shoe. If your foot is wider than the shoe, your toes will be pinched and you won't be able to wear those shoes for speedwalking (or for any extended walks, for that matter).

Winter walking. Lilian Rowen with a student speedwalking in Central Park. *Photo by Mel Levine*

COLD WEATHER WALKING

One of the most common excuses beginners give when they don't want to speedwalk is, "It's too cold!" I've been skiing since I was a child and I know that cold weather is no excuse for sitting home by the fire. Speedwalking in the winter is exhilarating, it can keep you in great shape, and it can reduce the cold weather doldrums that usually begin to set in after the Christmas holidays. For people with weight problems, winter exercise has one great advantage: It eliminates that annual ritual of self-loathing when spring and summer find you one size larger than your clothes. Learning to speedwalk in the winter takes only a little motivation, a little preparation, and some good advice.

    1. Begin speedwalking in the spring or fall, so that you're enthusiastic and your body is accustomed to the effort. It's much more difficult to begin an exercise in the dead of winter than it is when the weather is mild and you're enthusiastic about self-improvement.

2. Dress properly.
3. Warm up and cool down properly.

THE SPEEDWALKER'S COLD WEATHER UNIFORM

Dressing properly for winter activity is an art skiers learn early, or else they spend the season in the lodge instead of on the slopes. Layering is the key to staying warm, and it's especially important to learn this technique *before* you catch cold and opt for a season of slothful hibernation. Layering doesn't mean one bulky sweater over another until you weigh so much it's impossible to move. The theory behind layering is that several light layers trap warm air and act as a natural heating system with your own body warmth (remember, you will perspire even in cold weather). Another advantage to layering: You can discard extra outer layers as you warm up (but be careful to do this slowly and cautiously).

Your first layer should be absorbent and nonirritating—the basic cotton tee shirt, only you may choose a long-sleeved one for really cold days. Next, you should wear a shirt, wool sweater, or sweat shirt. You can add an extra layer—a parka, down vest, or coat—depending upon the temperature. Always keep in mind that your arms and torso need freedom of movement. Your outer wear should not be so tight or so bulky that your movement is restricted (down is a good choice since it's lightweight and very warm).

In addition, a wool scarf or a warm turtleneck sweater will prevent the heat from escaping from your layers, and keep your neck warm (stiff necks are often the results of chills—so always keep yours covered in cold weather).

On your legs you can start with a pair of cotton shorts, topped with sweat pants, although many people prefer to wear shorts over sweat pants. On really frigid days, long underwear or tights with the feet cut off are good ideas for an extra layer.

Feet, hands, and head are of the utmost importance. These extremities are often the first to feel the cold. If it's really frigid, you can get a painful case of frostbite when not properly protected. I always wear gloves when the temperature drops below fifty. Bare hands become chafed and sore. Many marathon runners wear inexpensive cotton painter's gloves in cool, but not really cold weather. Painter's gloves are a good idea, as they are inexpensive, practical, and can be discarded or folded up in a pocket along the way. When the temperature really dips into the thirties or below, I suggest a warm pair of wool mittens, which are warmer than gloves. Leather uppers on the mittens are practical, since you'll probably need to wipe your eyes or nose and wool can be irritating to the skin. If you continue to have a problem with cold hands, try a pair of skier's mittens; they're made of lightweight but very warm material and can last for many seasons.

Always cover your head. Over 40 percent of your body heat is lost through the head (yes, your mother was right!). A wool stocking cap or a parka with attached hood are two practical choices. When the weather is brisk but not cold enough to wear a hat, I stuff a bit of cotton in each ear. This prevents that cold feeling and helps to eliminate ear infections. Don't worry about not being able to hear. The cotton only mutes noise; you'll still be able to hear traffic, car horns, and voices. If you're especially sensitive to ear infections, or your ears are especially sensitive to the cold, wear the cotton in your ears under your hat—you'll stay toasty all winter.

To keep your feet from turning into chunks of ice, you'll want to layer your socks. I suggest a first layer of wool, since they stay warm and absorb perspiration, but if your feet are irritated by this, begin with properly fitting cotton socks, and then top them with a pair of wool ones. Make sure each layer is pulled up tightly and there are no bulges to blister and irritate your feet. Keeping your feet warm also protects your Achilles tendons and prevents muscle aches and cramps in your legs.

In addition, your face is bound to get red and chafed, especially when walking into the wind. You can wear a woolen ski mask, but many people find them uncomfortable (and unaesthetic). Other solutions: For women, a light layer of moisturizer followed by a protective makeup base is a good idea. Today more and more cosmetic companies are designing products for active, athletic women. Some even have sunscreen to protect your skin from the ravages of wind and sunburn. Men should moisturize too, and a thin layer of Vaseline over the face is good protection from biting winds. Take special care to apply protection to lips. Chap Stick, Blistex, or any lip coating should be tucked into a handy pocket. You'll probably need to reapply it as you walk.

Your eyes also suffer from winter weather. Glare from the snow and stinging winds can cause tears, blurred vision, and general discomfort. Ski goggles or good sunglasses will not only shade your eyes, they'll protect the delicate skin under the eyes and on the lids. Choose sunglasses or goggles carefully. First, they should fit properly. The last thing you need are glasses that slip, slide, and fall off. Many sunglasses simply don't protect your eyes from the blinding glare of the winter sun glinting off snow and ice. To check if they're really protective, try glasses on in the store. Look into the mirror. If you can see your eyes easily the lenses are probably too light (unless they're the photochromic kind that darken in the sun). The best lens colors are dark green, neutral gray, and brown. These colors filter the ultraviolet rays and provide glare protection without distorting the colors you see around you.

COLD WEATHER ALERT

Pay special attention to your warm-ups and cool-downs on wintery days. Warming up may take longer, as your muscles really are cold. Be sure to warm up indoors, making sure you aren't chilled or stiff before you begin (things will only get worse if you start off cold!). Begin speedwalking slowly; think of your body as an engine that needs to build up steam gradually. Soon you'll forget the temperature and your moving muscles will provide their own warmth and energy.

Cooling down in blustery weather can also be a bit tricky. If you stop exercising too abruptly, you risk becoming dizzy or fainting. Be sure not to discard too many layers as you walk; when you stop, your body will chill quickly and you risk muscle cramps or annoying stiffness. To cool down properly, walk normally for a few blocks or laps. You should feel your "internal engine" downshifting and cooling. Wait until you're indoors before you do all your cool-downs. Once you get into the routine of cold weather walking, you'll become more aware of just how long it takes for your body to cool down, and warm up. You'll also find that by experimenting with layers it's possible to avoid most of the bite of winter winds. Of course if there's four feet of snow on the ground and the governor has declared an emergency, you'll just have to wait until conditions improve. So stay inside, do your warm-ups and get-ready exercises, and think—spring!

HOT WEATHER WALKING

Believe it or not, more people complain about the heat and humidity than about the cold. And if you're reading this during the summer, you probably agree with them. Here are a few basic guidelines for summer speedwalkers:

1. On very hot days, try to time your walks early in the morning or after the sun has set.

2. Drink plenty of fluids (slowly, don't gulp) to replace what you lose when you perspire.

3. Wear clothes that reflect the sun—white and light colors.

4. Always cover your head when speedwalking in the hot sun.

5. Try to speedwalk on cool surfaces—avoid hot pavements and choose dirt, grass, or hard sand.

6. Be aware of sunburn and wear sunscreen if your skin is sensitive. Cover your shoulders by wearing a tee shirt.

7. If you are uncomfortable in warm weather, acclimate yourself to the heat slowly. Begin speedwalking in the spring and wear sweat pants and a sweat shirt (no rubber suits, please!). In this way your body becomes more efficient at sweating and doesn't lose great amounts of minerals and salts.

8. Slow your pace and curtail your walk if you begin to feel dizzy or nauseated.

9. Wear sunglasses to protect your eyes.

10. In addition to all these tips, here's one from the California Walkers: Wear a "wet head." Walk with a towel or terry hat that has been dipped in cold water. Keep it on your head as you walk. If you're lucky enough to pass a sprinkler, revive it with a splash of cold water!

NIGHT WALKING AND OTHER PROBLEMS

If you prefer to speedwalk after the sun has set, be careful of the route you choose. Ideally, it should be well-lighted. If this isn't possible, accustom yourself to the route in the daylight. Potholes, sidewalk cracks, curves, and turns may not seem problematic in the light of day, but at night they can become treacherous.

If you're walking on heavily trafficked roads, wear a reflecting parka, or attach reflecting tape to your shorts and tee shirt. When walking on a paved road, walk toward the traffic and try to stay on the shoulder rather than the pavement.

Women, especially in urban areas, should give some extra thought to security during night walks. I choose to walk with a few friends, and usually carry a whistle. Of course, it's always better to avoid deserted country roads or unpatrolled city parks. It's best to walk where there are other people, lights, and a general feeling of security.

Whether you walk in the morning or the evening, you will notice that people are curious about what you're doing, and sometimes they have funny ways of showing it. When I first began speedwalking, people often shouted, "Hey, what're you doing, can't you run?" As the sport has become more widely known, people usually run to catch up with me and ask me what I'm doing and how they can learn. If you're bothered by questions, hecklers, and curiosity seekers, here's a solution a friend of mine developed: She wears a simple tee shirt, which says SPEEDWALKER. The word is printed on the back, so that side-of-the-road hecklers can see it as she leaves them in the dust! It's such a good idea that many of the walkers in my clinic had them made up. Now everyone in our speedwalking area knows what we're doing, and how well we're doing it.

WHAT SHOULD I EAT?

There's no special diet for speedwalking, unless you're over-weight, undernourished, or a junk food junkie. Techniques like carbohydrate loading and megavitamin experimentation are really for marathon runners who put tremendous demands upon their bodies. As a speedwalker, you'll be exerting your-self and burning up calories, but you won't be depleting your-self of any vital nutritional requirements. Of course, if your diet consists of pretzels, potato chips, and cookies, with an occasional steak thrown in, you won't lose weight and you will tire easily. Similarly, cutting out any vital elements like carbo-hydrates or protein will result in a nutritional imbalance and general feelings of weakness.

If you really want to get in healthy, glowing shape, start from the inside out. Get your diet "together" by eliminating extra calories found in foods like sugary cereals, carbonated sodas, additive-laden snacks, canned foods, and frozen desserts. Check labels for extra salt, sugar, and chemicals you can't pronounce. Most important, get back to the basics—the basic four. Remember your health and home economics class in high school? The lessons you learned then about the basic four food groups still make the most sense.
- Fruits and vegetables
- Bread and cereals
- Milk and dairy products
- Meat, poultry, and fish
These four groups constitute the basics of a well-balanced diet.

Generally, you should have at least one serving from each group every day. With all the talk about zero carbohydrates, liquid proteins, the "Drinking Man's Diet," and other fads, it's difficult to remember that good nutrition isn't all that complicated. I find that most people simply eat too much, eat the wrong foods, and don't exercise enough. Some of them try to make up for it by loading down with vitamin pills, brewer's yeast, and lots of healthy sounding (and expensive) food supplements. Vitamins, brewer's yeast, and food supplements are fine along with a balanced diet, but they should never be substituted for one.

SPEEDWALKER'S SNACKS

Obviously, it's not a good idea to eat just before you exercise. This can cause cramps, nausea, and diarrhea, forcing you to interrupt your walk in search of the nearest bathroom. Nutritionist Dr. Nesrin Bingol, Associate Professor of Pediatrics, and Chief of Genetics Section, Maternal and Infant Care, New York Medical College, offers the following advice:

1. Your energy intake should be sufficient, so that you don't feel weak or hungry during exercise.

2. Your stomach and upper bowel should be empty when you speedwalk. Therefore, it's best to limit food intake two to three hours before exercise.

3. Avoid dehydration by drinking fluids.

4. The best meal for energy should be eaten two to three hours prior to your walk; it should be high in carbohydrate, low in fat, with lots of liquid, little bulk, and very little salt.

Dr. Bingol, a firm believer in physical fitness, practices what she preaches. In spite of her busy hospital schedule, she attends my fitness classes twice a week and is an enthusiastic runner and walker.

If you hate to exercise on a totally empty stomach, or you've planned your walk when it's impossible to wait as long as two hours after your last meal, a light snack, such as an apple or pear, contains energy-giving carbohydrates and shouldn't upset your stomach. Avoid citrus fruits, however, since the high acid content can cause unpleasant stomachaches.

You will notice that after a vigorous workout you're not anxious to eat right away. This is a natural reaction, as your body takes awhile to readjust. Do drink plenty of fluids to replace what you've lost in perspiration (but be careful to drink slowly, and avoid sugary, carbonated drinks). It might take as long as two hours after a vigorous walk until you feel your appetite coming back. Some people tell me they're hungry right away, but the majority say it takes at least forty-five minutes until they feel like eating again.

What's the best post-speedwalking snack? Something fresh, clean, and healthy—a crisp salad, lean poultry or fish, or some fresh fruit and cottage cheese. It's not a good idea to "reward yourself" with a heavy, fatty meal. Eating like this will weigh you down, and can affect your performance the next time out.

If you're a heavy smoker, or heavy coffee drinker, you'll have to cut down (and eliminate smoking eventually). Tobacco contains 500–600 known poisons, and studies have shown that one cigarette can increase your heart rate by twenty beats per minute. Similarly, coffee is a stimulant that can "wire you up" and cause stomach cramps, especially when combined with vigorous activity. By now, you're probably well aware of the dangers of cigarette smoking and excessive coffee drinking. You will notice, however, that as you keep up with regular speedwalking, you won't want these things for a very sensible reason—they detract from your hard-won feelings of vigor and health, and they can slow your speedwalking progress. So if you feel you're hopelessly addicted to that morning coffee and cigarette, try a forty-five-minute speedwalk—you'll soon forget the "pleasures" of nicotine and caffeine.

Healthy speedwalking snacks should be easy to prepare, readily available, and delicious. Since people are always asking me for some low-calorie, high-energy snacks, here's a list of foods that speedwalkers in my clinics prefer. These don't provide complete nutrition, but if these foods aren't part of your diet, why not try them? They're light, provide essential vitamins, proteins, and energy-producing carbohydrates—and they taste great too!

Sprouts

One woman in my clinic grows her own bean and alfalfa sprouts right in her apartment. She then makes delicious salads and low-calorie snacks (you can add sprouts to tuna fish or any other sandwich favorite). Any whole, unheated, unsprayed bean, grain, or seed can be sprouted, including corn, buckwheat, and sunflower seeds. According to nutrition expert Frances Goulart:

"All grains, seeds, and nuts in their natural state are foods of fitness, but when sprouted, they become the foods on which superperformances are built." Ms. Goulart goes on to explain that germination "releases a flood of enzymes and those enzymes digest your food, freeing your body's supply of enzymes to do the repair and maintenance jobs they were intended for. The result: they reduce stress and give you lots of energy."*

Liver

Although many people turn up their noses at the thought of liver, it's one of the all-time wonder foods. It contains more vitamin A than meats and other "main course" choices, plus it's filled with easily digestable iron. The editor of *Let's Live* magazine (March 1978) explains that "pound for pound there's no food which contains so many invaluable nutrients as liver— liver is one of the foods richest in vitamin B12, which has been found by various experiments to help develop energy and endurance, delay old age and senility, and help build resistance to disease."

Raisins

When you feel the need for something sweet, raisins are a

*Frances Sheridan Goulart, *Eating to Win, Food Psyching for the Athlete* (New York: Stein & Day, 1978), p. 61.

good way to satisfy the craving without filling up on white, processed sugar. They're high in minerals and energizing vitamins, and they taste better than sugary candy. I always carry a small box of these little energy pellets in my pocket. After a long speedwalk, I'm really not ready to eat anything heavier than raisins—and after finishing one tiny box, I feel restored and "rewarded."

Avocados

My California friends have been long-time aficionados of this sumptuous fruit. It's easily digestible and contains vitamins A, B, C, D, E, and K, plus seventeen different oils. There are hundreds of ways to eat avocados; you can stuff them, slice them in salads, or mix them into dips—be careful if you're trying to cut down on calories, though, because avocados, especially when combined with fattening additions, can run high in calories.

Apricots

Often called "the fruit of paradise," this high-energy snack can be eaten fresh or dried (the nutrients are actually increased in the drying process). They contain large amounts of vitamin A plus calcium, iron, and potassium. Apricots are a terrific low-calorie, high-energy snack that can be eaten before or after speedwalking.

Vegetable Juices

If you have a juicer at home, any combination of raw vegetables and fruits, such as carrot, celery, or apple, makes a low-calorie, filling, and fast-acting energy drink. And if you're trying to reduce, here's some good news from Shirley Ross, the author of Nature's Drinks.

"Raw juices taken before meals have a tendency to reduce the desire for fats, starches, and sweets, partially because, while solid food takes about four hours to assimilate into the system, raw juices are completely digested into the blood-stream in twenty minutes."*

So after a speedwalk, when you're thirsty and need a lift, try concocting your own blend of vegetable and/or fruit juice. It's a healthy way to replace fluid and provide good solid nutrition!

These are just some of the healthy, natural, energy-giving foods that speedwalkers like to eat. You'll notice that I haven't mentioned fatty meats or starchy "extras." That's because, ounce for ounce, they can't provide the nutrition found in fresh vegetables, fruits, and lean poultry and fish.

Experiment with what feels right in your body. Try some of the speedwalker's snacks and add more fruits and vegetables to your diet. Remember not to eat or drink heavily before you speedwalk, and keep track of the foods that seem to give you increased energy, while you gradually eliminate those that slow you down.

WHAT ABOUT WEIGHT LOSS?

There's really only one way to lose weight—cut calories while you exercise.

Everyone wants to be thin, but losing weight without developing good muscle tone results in a skinny, shriveled look. I don't suggest you go on a new and rigorous diet at the same time you begin speedwalking. If you've been inactive for some time, it's best to adjust to your new routine gradually. Any dramatic change in eating habits can upset your equilibrium. As a result, I suggest a moderate program of weight loss—about two pounds a week.

Dr. Nesrin Bingol explains it this way: "The best way to reduce body weight is by reducing body fat to a healthy minimum. But fat loss should not exceed a rate of three pounds each week—a two-pound weekly loss is actually more desir-

*Shirley Ross, Nature's Drinks; Recipes for Vegetable and Fruit Juices, Teas and Coffees (New York: Vintage Books, 1974), p. 9.

able. More rapid weight loss can involve loss of muscle mass and this is not compatible with effective training or with performance in sports such as speedwalking."

Remember, your body is not a slot machine. Just because you've cut down on calories, don't expect to lose weight immediately—it takes time. You will discover, however, that with regular, vigorous speedwalking you'll be able to eat sensibly without starving. That's because once your body becomes attuned to constant workouts, it becomes more efficient at burning up calories. Even more important, you become less interested in consuming extra ones. You become more attracted to low-calorie, high-energy foods because they improve your performance and help you maintain that glowing, healthy feeling throughout the day.

One woman in my clinic explains her "weight problem" this way:

"Believe me, there wasn't a diet or a slimming regime that I hadn't tried. This had been going on for so long, I'd actually forgotten what normal eating was really like. Then a friend dragged me along for one of Lilian's speedwalking clinics and exercise classes. I began to enjoy the speedwalking. I didn't think of it just as a way to lose weight; I needed to get out of the house and this exercise was easy, undemanding, and a perfect excuse for spending some time by myself.

"After a while, I noticed that my appetite diminished after the longer speedwalks. I increased my time, and my interest in cake and sweets (my undoing) decreased accordingly. Then I went on a simple, low-calorie, balanced diet. I found that I could eat normally—three square meals a day—and not be hungry and not gain weight.

"Before, I had always used exercise as a punishment and had combined it with a really low-calorie, low-carbohydrate diet. No wonder I was an exercise-hater! Now, I'm finally free from my obsession with diets. I speedwalk every day, eat normally, and I look and feel better than I have in years."

Don't speedwalk to "work off a piece of cake." Walk the mile and skip the cake. And as Dr. Dorothy Harris states in *WomenSports* Magazine: "Physical activity charts that offer exercise and weight loss formulas—like walking one hour to burn 123 calories or running one hour to burn 600 calories—can be rather discouraging. However, all the evidence supports the fact that regular vigorous activity decreases fat storage over time. The important thing to remember is that to make any difference in the proportion of body fat, one must exercise on a regular basis with the effort sufficiently intense and sustained over a period of time. Those who exercise are significantly leaner than their sedentary counterparts. And although that leanness may not necessarily be translated into weight loss, loss of fat is important for total body conditioning—unless one is a pearl diver."*

FOOTNOTES

Oh, those aching feet! You pinch them in confining shoes, you stand on them all day, and now you're expected to speedwalk on them! If your feet hurt, chances are your back hurts, and your legs and ankles ache too. Proper foot care can't be stressed enough. Your feet are important to your posture and balance, and to your future as a speedwalker. Strong, healthy feet can help you feel energized all day long. If your feet ache after speedwalking or intermittently during the day, check your everyday footwear as well as your running shoes. Remember, high heels are killers, but so are shoes that are too pointed or squared-off. Make sure you're wearing the proper running shoes—ones that are flexible and fit properly, with springy soles. Once you've checked your footwear, it's time to begin whipping those feet into speedwalking shape. Here are a few easy exercises that can be done just about anywhere or any-time. If you have a few minutes of privacy during the day, they can be done at your desk.

*WomenSports, "Fat, No Deposit, No Return." October 1977, p. 54.

1. The Outside Roll

Stand with your bare feet about shoulder width apart. Roll onto the outside of your feet. Slowly raise yourself on your toes. Roll back onto the inside of your feet and return by placing your weight on your heels. Do this slowly three times. You should feel those muscles working!

2. Pencil Pick Up

Place a pencil on the floor and try to pick it up with your bare foot. Raise that foot and hold the pencil to a count of five—really grip with your toes. This also improves balance. Return the pencil to the floor and repeat with your other foot.

3. Toe Fan

Stand up, feet slightly apart. Try to separate your toes, by spreading them out like a fan. Do this without lifting your toes off the ground. At first this may seem difficult; that's because most people don't use the muscles in and around the toes. But these are voluntary muscles, and you can learn to control them. If you separate your fingers at the same time, you'll find that the exercise is easier to do. Once you've learned how to "fan your toes," practice this simple exercise each morning before you put on your shoes and each evening when you take them off. After a while you'll be stretching and strengthening your toes automatically.

4. The Arch Enhancer

If you have weak or "fallen" arches, this is a must! Sit on the floor, braced on your hands, with your elbows bent. Bring your

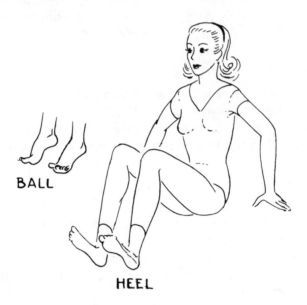

BALL

HEEL

knees close to your chest and place both heels on the floor. Now change your foot position so that the balls of your feet are resting on the floor. Keep changing from heels to balls, slowly straightening your knees almost out as you "walk forward." Walk backward in the same manner. Your body should not move, only your legs will do the walking. You should feel this in your shins, calves, and arches.

SPIKE HEEL FIGHTERS

It you've been wearing spike heels for any length of time, you've probably got plenty of foot problems. The best way to deal with them is to go barefoot or to wear low heels as often as possible. Try wearing a medium heel to work, and then change to flats as soon as you come home. What is the best medicine for women who have been tripping around town in four-inch heels? An hour a day in bare feet. Here are two exercises that will help you strengthen and stretch muscles that are weak and tight.

1. The Place Walk

Walk in place—two steps on your toes, two steps on your heels. Keep alternating. You should feel this in your hamstring and calf muscles.

2. The Forward Lean

Stand with your feet parallel, making sure they are shoulder width apart. Bend both knees and push them forward and

downward, as if you were skiing. Bounce gently. Hold for a count of twenty.

REPEAT BOTH EXERCISES TWICE DAILY. If you need additional "Spike Heel Fighters," concentrate on the "Runner's Stretch" and on "The A Frame" on pp. 66 and 79.

STRESS, SPEEDWALKING, AND YOU

Stress is a natural by-product of life in the twentieth century. Although stress is psychological in origin, it's often experienced as physical. Tension in your back, a knot in your stomach, and muscle cramps can all be attributed to increased pressure and tension. In addition, extreme stress can contribute to ulcers, migraine headaches, asthma, and a host of other serious ailments. There is no simple formula for completely eliminating stress from your daily life. Some stress can actually help you "gear up" for your job, for sports, or for handling demanding decisions and problems in your personal life. Too much stress can hamper your effectiveness, too little can detract from your motivation. The trick, obviously, is to keep stress within manageable limits—and to avoid becoming its victim.

Sports are a healthy way to release tension and minimize the negative effects of stress. They can distract you and ease you into a gentle rhythmic pace. In addition, speedwalking increases your circulation, and enables your body to use oxygen more efficiently, helping your brain and your psyche to function more effectively. Nondemanding and noncompetitive, speedwalking helps you to release anxiety, anger, and frustration. Once you begin to free yourself from the unpleasant side effects of stress, you can lose yourself and think a problem through. Allowing yourself to "let go" and become lost in the rhythm of your own pace has a gentle, almost hypnotic effect. Once mastered, it's more effective and a healthier tension reliever than an afternoon drink or a tranquilizer.

THE SPEEDWALKER'S
THREE-STAGE RELAXING FORMULA

When your stomach is in a knot, your back is hunched over, and your muscles are contracted and rigid, it's best not to jump into your speedwalking clothes and hit the track—at least not until you've allowed a little extra time for this special three-stage relaxing formula. These tension relieving exercises should be done before warm-ups, or any time you feel the knotting, twisting effects of stress. Think of these easy exercises as a natural tranquilizers, and use them freely at any time during the day. They will help you to keep your body loose, flexible, and fit, and to control the rhythm of your breathing as you speedwalk. This not only reduces tension, it helps to ease those unattractive frowns and furrows that appear during times of stress (and sometimes become permanent!).

The three-stage relaxing formula consists of the following three steps:

- Release muscle tension.
- Control breathing cycle.
- Control mental imagery.

Stage One: Release Muscle Tension

Find a quiet comfortable place where you will not be disturbed, and where there is soft lighting, or where you can lie still in total darkness. Lie down on your back, so that you are as comfortable as possible. Slowly scrunch up your forehead and tighten your jaw. Now, let your face go slack. Next, tense your shoulders and then relax them and let them drop. Continue this tensing and relaxing with every part of your body. Make a fist, relax, and let your hand go limp. Tighten arms, release the muscles. Tense and relax every part of your body right on down to your toes. Concentrate on the muscles as you do this, and visualize the stress literally being "squeezed" from your body.

Stage Two: Control Breathing Cycle

Still remaining in this same position, concentrate on controlling your breathing. Inhale through your nose to a slow count of six. Hold your breath to a count of six. Now, exhale through your mouth to a slow count of eight. Try to force the air out of your lungs and to lose yourself in the sound and the rhythm of your own breathing. Next, increase your count to seven (inhale), seven (hold the breath), nine (exhale), and then eight, eight, ten.

Stage Three: Control Mental Imagery

Once you have finished the breathing exercise, remain in the same position and close your eyes. Picture yourself walking along a clean white beach (or in the mountains or some other peaceful quiet place). Visualize the ocean gently rolling against the shore and try to feel the cool pleasant breeze as it brushes against your face. Picture yourself inhaling the fresh sea air and walking briskly as you effortlessly heel-toe into a rhythmic speedwalk. Continue with this peaceful picture until you feel relaxed enough to open your eyes. Don't get up from your position too quickly. Wait until you feel the results of the relaxing formula. The tension and knots in your muscles should be released. You should have a peaceful picture of yourself to help alleviate the stress you were feeling before you began. Rest comfortably for a few minutes before you resume your daily activities or before you begin your warm-ups.

COFFEE BREAK RELAXER

Having a tough day? Do you feel the beginning signs of stress at your job, at school, or at home? If you don't have time for the three-stage relaxing formula, here's a mini-relaxer that you can do just about anytime and anywhere.

Sitting in a chair, let your head drop forward, chin to chest. Then raise your head and let it drop backward. Let your jaw go slack. Raise your head and let it drop forward once again. Circle one shoulder backward, then the other. Repeat several times. Shrug both shoulders. Now separate your feet and drop your chin to your chest again. Drop your shoulders and arms forward and bend down between your knees as far as possible. Don't force or push. Remain in this position one to two minutes. Slowly return to an upright position. Do this three times.

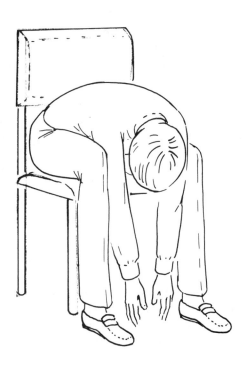

JUST FOR WOMEN

Menstruation and menopause are the "big two" for most women. They're afraid to exercise, they're worried about hurting themselves, or they have been convinced that a woman simply doesn't exercise during "these times." Of course, if your physician has advised you to eliminate exercise for a real physical reason, that's something else. Otherwise, don't use the "big two" as little reasons for sitting home on an ever-widening backside.

MENSTRUATION

Exercise during this time can be the cure, rather than the cause of cramps and discomfort. More and more women athletes are proving that menstruation (and in some cases, even pregnancy) is no impediment to an active exercise schedule. Dorothy Hamill, the 1976 Olympic gold medal figure skating champion, recently disclosed that in 1974 she won the National Figure Skating Championship while she was having her menstrual period.

Dedicated runners, swimmers, and skiers seldom alter or discontinue rigorous training schedules during "that time" of the month. Although you may not compare yourself to a professional athlete, this evidence should indicate that menstruation is *not* an illness and *not* a reason to "take to bed." Indeed, many menstrual problems (everything, from swelling to nausea and cramps, is called "dysmenorrhea") can be substantially lessened and even eliminated by moderate, unstressful exercise. Medical studies strongly point to the conclusion that some forms of dysmenorrhea are closely related to improper amounts of oxygen in the body and to a decreased flow of oxygen-carrying blood to internal organs. In addition, improved circulation plus the gentle strengthening of abdominal muscles that takes place during speedwalking, can reduce bloated feelings as well as lower back pain.

As for "menstrual blues," why not take your blue feelings for a walk and lose them along the way? Moodiness, irritability, and stress can worsen cramps and make you dread your period. A brisk speedwalk will make you feel good about yourself, get your circulation going, and remind you that it really is great to be a woman!

If you bleed heavily the first few days of your period, walk slower than you normally would, wear an extra tampon or sanitary napkin, and be sure to adjust the length and intensity of your workout to a sensible rate. You will notice, as the months pass, that your body adapts more and more to increased exercise. Stomach muscles will become stronger and your back will ache less. And if you practice the relaxing and tension relieving exercises, you'll be less "uptight" about that time of the month.

SUGGESTIONS FOR SPEEDWALKING DURING MENSTRUATION

1. Start toning and strengthening stomach muscles before you get your period. Remember, strong stomach muscles help relieve back pain too. Concentrate on these stomach strengtheners from the get-ready exercises: "The High Roller," the "Semi-Sit-Up," the "Spread Eagle," and "The Total Sit-Up."

2. If you are reluctant to engage in a vigorous speedwalk, why not try some variety walking or practice the Mexican mobile exercises. This will give you the benefits of movement, but at a more controlled pace.

3. If you are suffering from mild cramps, reduce the hip swivel and concentrate on your heel-toe movement and your arm swing.

4. Exercise daily *before* your period and be sure to take time out for the three-stage relaxing formula when the stress and tension of premenstrual syndrome begin to appear.

MENOPAUSE

Many women think they're "too old to exercise." They really believe the myths that menopause signals the end of an active life. The truth is that most women begin menopause around age fifty, and they have a life expectancy of at least seventy-five. That leaves twenty-five years in which you can resign yourself to feeling like "an old lady" or twenty-five years in which you can try to feel and look as fit and healthy as possible.

Menopause involves a series of hormonal changes. Exercise that is regular, safe, and easy can help you cope with both the physical and psychological effects of those changes. As estrogen levels begin to drop, your body gradually looses calcium. This causes bones to become brittle and porous, a condition known as "osteoporosis." When osteoporosis develops, women can become more prone to injury and a simple fall can result in a broken bone. But an exercise like speedwalking, that is safe and progressive, can help give your bones and muscles the stimulation they need to ward off the more deteriorating effects of calcium loss.

Dr. Dorothy Harris explains it this way: "Since activity stimulates bone maintenance, the way to stave off osteoporosis is to continue a physically active life-style."*

Loss of calcium isn't the only change you experience during menopause. Lowered estrogen levels often affect cholesterol levels. An increase in cholesterol and a decrease in activity can result in heart disease. A careful diet combined with regular exercise can lower your chances of cardiovascular problems as you grow older.

Skin tone and condition can also be affected by decreased estrogen production. Although nothing can prevent wrinkling, exercise can tighten flabby muscles and improve circulation. This will help you to retain the glow and texture of your complexion.

But aside from the physical benefits, speedwalking will help

*WomenSports, February 1978, p. 55.

you to realize that menopause hasn't curtailed your ability to lead an active life, and that the normal changes that take place during this time need not be debilitating. The easy, rhythmic pace of speedwalking combined with the important fact that your feet never leave the ground, which eliminates the pounding and jolting of most sports, make it an ideal exercise for women who want to stay in the swing of things—safely.

SUGGESTIONS FOR EXERCISE DURING MENOPAUSE

1. "Dowager's Hump" is an awful name for a common condition that can develop with middle age. Here's a two-part exercise to help prevent this from happening to you!

a) Lie on your stomach, arms extended at shoulder level,

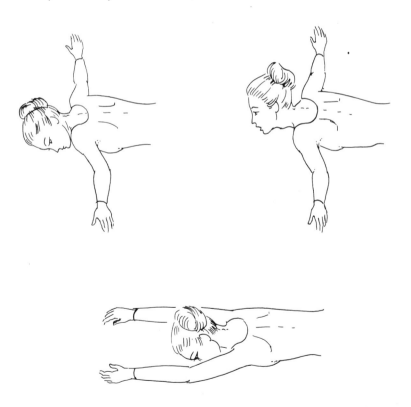

head resting on one cheek. Slowly lift your head and bring it back as far as you can and turn it onto the other cheek. Do this eight times each day.

b) Begin in the same position. Raise both your arms and your head simultaneously. Bring your arms together in front of your head while you slowly turn your head onto the other cheek. Open your arms again and turn your head the other way. Open and close four times. Do this daily.

2. If you've been sedentary, try variety walking and the Mexican mobile exercises before you begin vigorous workouts.

3. Concentrate on hip girdle and shoulder flexibility by practicing these exercises from the get-ready program: "Waist Twister," "The Bridge," "The Swinger," "The Swivel," "The Arm Crisscross."

JUST FOR MEN

Women aren't the only ones with "special problems." In general, men have a higher ratio of muscle to fat than do women. Their muscles are usually stronger and their ligaments are tighter. The result: Most men are physically more powerful than women (there are exceptions, of course), but they are usually less flexible. I've noticed these flexibility inequities in my exercise classes. Fewer men than women can touch their toes, sit cross-legged, or complete many of the stretches. Like strength, however, flexibility can be improved. It's important for men, especially older men, who are even more inflexible than their younger counterparts, to achieve desired flexibility. Here are a few flexibility enhancers that should be practiced daily. You'll notice that "old stiffness" will begin to disappear in no time at all!

BEGIN ALL FLEXIBILITY SESSIONS WITH THE TOTAL RELAXERS (see p. 27). THESE WILL PREPARE YOUR MUSCLES FOR STRETCHING AND PREVENT "PULLS" OR STRAINS.

1.The Long Back Stretch

Lie on your back. Put your right foot on top of your left knee, while your right arm stretches overhead. Bring your right knee gently toward the floor on your left side. At the same time press it down with your left hand. Hold the knee in this position for a count of ten. Keep both shoulders on the floor at all times. Repeat with the opposite leg. Do this three times, alternating sides.

2.The Hamstringer

Lie on your back in the basic position. Bring right knee as close to your chest as possible. Extend right leg toward the ceiling, pointing your toe. Lock your knee and lower your right leg to

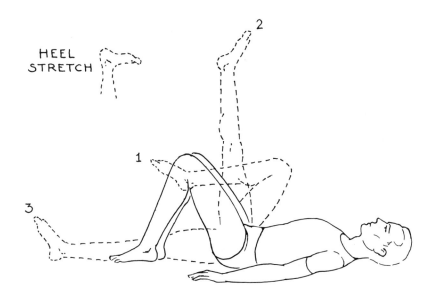

HEEL STRETCH

the floor. Slide the leg back to the starting position. Repeat with the left leg. Now repeat with heel stretch three times each leg alternately.

3.Double Heel Stretch

Same starting position as in "Single Heel Stretch" from get-ready exercises, pp. 30–31. Bring both knees to your chest. Your hands should remain under your buttocks. Stretch both heels up toward the ceiling. Straighten your legs out as much as possible. Hold to a count of three. Now bend both knees and relax. Do this six times. This stretch will be felt in the backs of your knees. To increase the stretch, bring your knees closer to your chest.

4.The Flat Back

Stand directly in front of a table. Place your arms and hands on the table and walk backward until you can bend over while your back remains straight. Your back and arms will now be parallel to the floor. Let your head hang downward toward the floor. Feel that stretch in your shoulder and pectoral muscles!

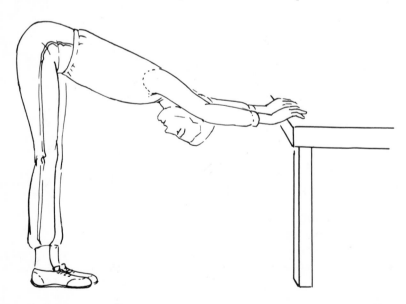

Hold this position for a slow count of twenty. This is also a good exercise for anyone interested in loosening shoulders for race walking.

5. The Fold Over

Sit up and place your legs straight ahead. Place your chin to your chest and grasp your legs as close to your ankles as possible. Pull your body downward gently by bending your elbows. Hold to a count of ten.

CREATING A SPECIAL SPEEDWALKING PROGRAM FOR YOUR SPECIAL NEEDS

This chapter might not have answered all your questions, but we hope it helped. The idea is to develop a program that suits your needs and your abilities. Work with the information in this chapter. Experiment with some of these hints, solutions, and special tips. You'll probably find that many things that prevented you from regular exercise in the past really aren't problems after all. Remember, speedwalking should be made to fit into your life, not vice versa. If you're not sure your solutions are the best ones, try experimenting with them. You'll know what's right for you when it feels right and it makes you feel great. Don't use your age, the weather, or a little bit of tension or stress as reasons for depriving yourself of a simple, enjoyable way to improve your health, your looks, and your outlook on life!

8.
THE PAYOFF

Once you've become involved in, and dedicated to, your program of speedwalking, you'll begin to reap the benefits. Like a blue chip stock, speedwalking will bring you dividends every day you stick with it. If you've shied away from exercise all your life, speedwalking will not only transform the way you look and feel, but also the way you think. Increased self-confidence comes with body awareness—the realization that you really can "do it," and that doing it doesn't involve pain, injury, or sacrifice. If you're a running dropout, speedwalking gives you a sport to fill the exercise void. It offers you the benefits of a sport *and* a conditioning exercise. And if you're really enthusiastic, you can move forward into the competitive world of race walking. The special appendix on pp. 138–144 gives you all the basics you'll need to begin intensive training.

Speedwalking is not just another exercise. There are "extra benefits"—payoffs that you may have never considered:

1. *An enhanced sense of rhythm and grace* that will be transferred to your everyday walking and moving.

2. *A natural, healthy method of modifying food intake* and controlling your weight.

3. *A body that is not only trim, but shapely, firm, and supple.*

4. *A network of friends and a "support system"* that can help you achieve your athletic goals, and encourage you to break through the barriers of defeatism.

5. *A natural tranquilizer,* one that can be mixed freely with your life-style, your needs, and your abilities. Speedwalking is an effective and healthy way to handle stress, deal with depression, and release the pent-up emotions that might have caused distressing physical symptoms.

6. *A way to know yourself better.* Long speedwalks give you time alone with yourself, time to organize your thoughts, think things through, and make important (and not-so-important) decisions.

7. *A new direction in life.* Finally, and most important, speedwalking will put you on a new path. It will allow you to prove to yourself that *you can do it.* Working from the inside out, speedwalking will change the way you feel about yourself, and this is the extra ingredient that will improve your performance and enhance your determination. An improved self-image can lead to lots more than better and faster speedwalking times—it can lead to a whole new direction in life, one that's built on confidence, strength, optimism, and health. And after all, isn't that what self-improvement is all about?

The payoff in speedwalking is up to you. The benefits can be rich and enduring and they can last a lifetime. Speedwalking has added a new dimension to my life. I hope you'll allow it to do the same for you.

APPENDIX: *MOVING FORWARD: RACE WALKING*

Race walking is actually the parent of speedwalking. A sport with a long history and tradition, race walking has been traced back as far as medieval England. When you think about it, you can understand why this sport has been in existence for so long—it's a natural outgrowth of walking. The unique swivel-hipped movement of race walkers making their way around tracks and alongside roadways has been, and continues to be, a common sight in Europe and most recently, in the United States.

Although race walking has undergone some changes, it's essentially the same sport that was introduced to the Olympic games of 1908. Since that time, race walking legends like George Larner of Great Britain and Ugo Frigerio of Italy have impressed the world community of athletes with their style, form, and stamina, *and* with their incredible times.

In the 1920s, race walking became the vogue in the United States. Six-day walking races in Madison Square Garden were attended by crowds of cheering fans. Later, race walking seemed to go "underground" in this country, though it continued to flourish in Europe. Now, once again, race walkers have begun to dot the landscape of America's tracks, roadways, and jogging paths. World's records, once held by Swedes and

Englishmen, are now being challenged by a new crop of determined American race walkers. In the popular New York City marathon, thirty-five Olympic-hopeful race walkers finished the race right alongside (and many, way before) the runners. Carl Schueler of Washington, D.C., completed the arduous course in three hours, forty-seven minutes, and thirty seconds. This incredible time actually put him *ahead* of more than six thousand runners!

It's no surprise that race walking is being rediscovered by an athletically conscious America. As the running injuries begin to mount, race walking becomes more and more the choice of men and women who want the challenge of a competitive and demanding sport without the risks. If you've progressed in your speedwalking, you might be interested in "moving forward" into the competitive and more strenuous sport of race walking.

Although speedwalking is an adaptation of race walking, it doesn't require the same type of strength and power. By watching race walkers in action you will be able to see for yourself the great force exerted in their arm, hip, and leg movements. Race walkers move quickly. With economy of movement and the flexibility and strength of their arms, shoulders, and hip girdle, they make this a tough and demanding sport. Although race walking uses the same basic heel-toe technique as speedwalking, it concentrates on vigorous arm thrusts and an unusual pelvic movement. To race walk properly, you'll need strength and flexibility as well as stamina and endurance.

Speedwalking is probably the best way to prepare yourself for race walking. The body conditioning you'll be getting in the get-ready exercises, warm-ups, and cool-downs, and in speedwalking itself, will prime you for the demands of this sport. Although they are similar, there are some differences between speedwalking and race walking. Mainly they are differences of intensity and style. When you speedwalk, you swivel your hips, but when you race walk, your hip is *rotated downward and forward.* If you observe race walkers in action, you'll see that the hip drops as the back leg drives forward.

The rotation and drop can be felt in the pelvic girdle and it gives your body the power for the forward thrusting movement so evident in high-speed race walking.

Another important aspect of race walking is the arm motion. In order to keep the body moving properly, your arms should drive forward. Obviously this type of power requires a strong upper body and increased flexibility in the shoulder girdle area.

When race walking, your arms should be bent at a 90 degree angle and they should move through an arc with your hands

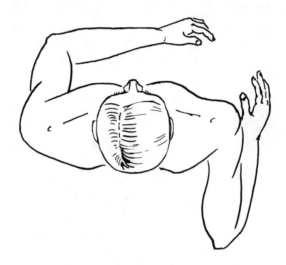

reaching no farther back than the ball joint of the hip (this can be measured by the vertical seam in the side of your shorts) nor higher than the middle of your chest.

Rather than relaxing, your hands should be loosely clenched. Shoulders must remain down and stationary. Strong arms, shoulders, and backs can propel most race walkers across finish lines even when their feet and legs have tired out.

Here's an extra arm-strengthener suggested by John Kelley, California race walking champion:

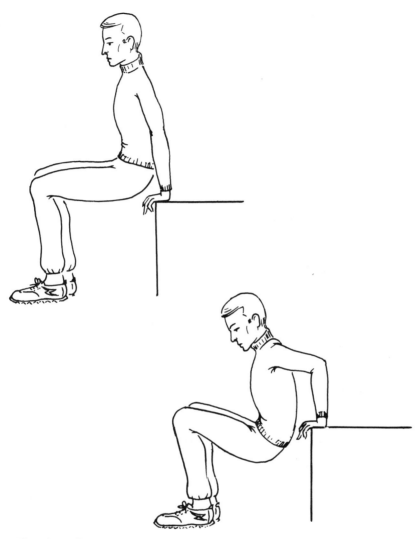

The Arm Pump

Place both arms behind you, elbows straight, brace yourself on a sturdy chair or bench, both knees bent. Now bend both elbows, so that your body is lowered well below bench level and come up again by straightening your elbows. Pump up and down at least ten times.

COMMON ERRORS

Race walking can be difficult and demanding. But as you progress with speedwalking, you'll be building all the qualities necessary for race walking. Although this sport should come fairly naturally to you after you've been speedwalking for a few months, here are a few tips and common errors you should be aware of:

1. *Don't hold your arms too high.* This can be observed when your arms are tense and pumping so vigorously that your elbows are bent at more than a 90 degree angle.

2. *Don't tilt your head too far forward or back.* You'll feel tension in your upper back and chest and you'll pull your trailing foot away too soon.

3. *Observe your foot placement.* As in speedwalking, be on the alert for feet that don't come down in a straight line. This leads to lifting and bouncing.

4. *Avoid any excessive forward or backward lean.* Very much like speedwalking, race walking requires that you hold your head and trunk in a nearly upright position.

5. *Avoid lifting your feet off the ground.* Race walking judges are very strict about flaws such as "creeping," walking with bent knees, and "lifting," walking or bouncing with both feet leaving the ground. Unbroken contact with the ground at all times is not only a strict rule of the sport, it improves the quality and speed of movement and helps to prevent injury.

LEARN BY OBSERVING

The hip drop that is such an essential aspect of race walking must be seen in order to be fully understood. In this photograph you can see the difference between speedwalking and race walking. Note Roger Brandwein, on the left. An Olympic

Roger Brandwein's racewalking style contrasts with Lilian Rowen's less exaggerated speedwalking stride. *Photo by Kurt Meissner*

race walking hopeful, Roger has won several competitions due to his perfect form and powerful body. You can actually see his hip drop and his arms pump as he race walks. You'll be seeing lots more people like Roger race walking and competing throughout the country. As joggers become injured and drop out, they have increasingly turned to this sport for competition that is challenging, strenuous, and safe. Many Y's, Road Runners, and Race Walkers clubs are staging competitions and enlisting the coaching help of trained race walkers. Race walking clinics and classes are being arranged by coaches, experienced walkers, and interested beginners. If you want the opportunity to compete, race walking marathons and mini-marathons are becoming as popular as well-publicized running races. In addition, race walking has been included in the Junior Olympics (it's great for kids!) and will be an event in the Pan American and Olympic games. Finding a good coach and enlisting the participation of your speedwalking friends is all you need to form your own race walking group and to work on the fine points of your form and technique. If you've advanced with your speedwalking, all you need is some encouragement, added strength and flexibility, and the determination to stick with it. You'll find that race walking is the sport of the future, and one that will ensure you a lifetime of fitness.

BOOKS ON RACE WALKING

Racewalk to Fitness by Howard Jacobson (New York: Simon and Schuster, 1980).

"Racewalking" (a pamphlet) by Martin Rudow (Mt. View, CA.: World Publications, 1975). This is an excellent, easy-to-read, well-illustrated guide. It's inexpensive and distributed by Runner's World magazine. It should be all you need to train and to prepare for competition.